MW01490116

ESCAPE
From Abuse

Til Hageer

Reboot Your Thinking
Reboot Your Life

TESTIMONIALS

"Til Hagen has tackled the demoralizing practice of abuse that squelches the spirits of dynamic individuals. It need not continue if we choose otherwise. Embrace Til's thoughts and advice. Read carefully with your mind and heart to hear the hope that she offers. It is our choice. Turn up the light and the darkness disappears."

- Loren Murfield, Ph.D.
Murfield International
Odessa, Florida

"Til Hagen's process has enabled me to look at life differently, to accept some of the bad things and move on. With her help, my life has improved tremendously!"

- Abuse survivor

"Til Hagen's positive outlook on life after many years of adversity, is inspiring."

- Anneke Gorter
Program Chairman Women's Group
Bentveld, Holland

"Til Hagen's ideas motivate and give strength to go ahead and do the things that need to be done in spite of the adversity in the past."

- Sandra McIntosh
Unity of Brandon
Brandon, Florida

"Ms.Til's approach to life is that everyone has a right to be happy, and happiness is found within ourselves. She shows how to respect our feelings and thoughts and not to look back."

- Abuse survivor

"Til Hagen is inspiring and motivational, humorous and engaging."

- Rev. Peggie Marks
Spiritual Director
St. Petersburg, Florida

"Til's words answer many questions."

- Rev. Virginia Leicht
Minister Unity in the Grove
Lakeland, Florida

"I am pleased to recommend Til Hagen's work without reservation!"

- Jan Falcione
Director of Development and Marketing
Mary and Martha House
Ruskin, Florida

THE 5-Step PROCESS TO

ESCAPE From Abuse

Reboot Your Thinking
Reboot Your Life

by **TIL HAGEN**, M.Ed.

Foreword by T. Michael Ingram, Ph.D.

The 5-Step Process to Escape from Abuse
Copyright © 2011 by Til Hagen. All rights reserved.

Published by: Wooden Shoe Press
www.tilhagen.com

Edited by: Denise McCabe | www.mccabeediting.com
Book cover design and formatting: Eli Blyden | www.CrunchTimeGraphics.net

Printed in the United States of America.

ISBN 13: 978-1-4276-5140-2

1. Self-Help. 2. Abuse. 3. Adult Abuse Victims–United States

ACKNOWLEDGMENTS

I could never have written this book without the support of the women I interviewed. They have my deepest gratitude.

Then to several other people I owe a special and heartfelt thanks:

First to Dr. T. Michael Ingram, the wonderful psychologist who made me "whole" again. Without you I would not be where I am today.

Then to my editor, Denise McCabe, who went above and beyond the call of duty to get this book written and to Robyn Winters whose input was invaluable. I love you both!

To my husband, Adrian Hagen, my one true love, who drafted several book designs and whose enthusiasm and unfailing support with "computer glitches" helped me finish this book.

Lastly, to my son, Mike Vangroll, who is so proud of his mom having written a book.

TABLE OF CONTENTS

FOREWORD

Til Hagen has had a difficult journey. She has faced various forms of abuse with her determination to survive, and in fact, she has courageously overcome them with the resilience to thrive. In doing so she has learned and grown from her experiences. In addition, she has written a book that is just one part of a larger contribution that she continues to make by speaking out against the emotional/verbal and sexual abuse perpetrated on women.

The book is written in terms that a layperson can understand. It speaks to the need for the issue of abuse to be heard, and to the ways of healing that other victims can actually apply to their own lives. It also provides helpful examples of how anyone, at any age, can face the challenges of change, and grow into a self-confident human being. She speaks from the heart, mind, and soul!

Til tells of having been in therapy for Post Traumatic Stress Disorder (PTSD). She has learned about the diagnoses and treatments for abuse and PTSD, and applied what she discovered in therapy to her own life. Now she is offering these wise learnings to others who have similar issues.

Til has experienced intense fear and vivid flashbacks – not an unusual occurrence with PTSD – where she was regularly reliving her past incidences. She was anxious and constantly afraid that the next thing she was going to hear would be cruel and hurtful. She boldly figured out how to guard against those situations.

Til Hagen writes from experience. She knows that abuse can have traumatic consequences leading to a stress level that is damaging both physically and mentally.

Following her five-step program to resolve this stress shifts the focus away from re-experiencing the trauma to adopting positive actions that can be taken to resolve the issue of abuse.

- T. Michael Ingram, Psy.D.
Seffner Clinic
Seffner, Florida
2011

INTRODUCTION

Sometimes life throws us surprises when we least expect them, and it is up to us to learn how to deal with them. This happened to me when, after a lifetime of abuse and two failed marriages, I was introduced to my present husband to whom I have now been happily married for more than 16 years. Trust and acceptance that something good was coming my way, after all those lonely years, were very difficult for me to accept, but his patience and kindness finally made me realize that this was the real thing. I could let go of the knot in my stomach!

However, there was still a lot of anger and stress, suppressed for so many years, and after a bout with Post Traumatic Stress Disorder, I needed, and received, help. Afterwards I realized that, based upon my own experiences, I had developed a 5-step process that enabled me to become a confident, strong, and loving person. Because I "had been there" and "done that," I could, and should, help others, and so I became an inspirational speaker, teacher, and writer.

In Chapter 1 of this book I will relate some of my own abusive experiences, such as my childhood, my life in the workplace, my two marriages, and the abuse of two of my children. Chapters 3 through 7 deal with the various kinds of emotional and verbal abuse. Chapter 8 describes various forms of sexual abuse. Each chapter has five stories of people who dealt with a particular type of abuse, unconsciously using the 5-step process I have identified and developed.

This book is designed to be small enough that it can be easily slipped in to a purse. It is my fervent hope that when victims of abuse read it, they will find the courage to use it.

Chapter One

OPENING THE SCREEN TO THE LIFE OF AN ABUSE SURVIVOR

"How dare you, you stupid girl!" he screamed. "All Fs! Don't you have any brains?" Then more choice words, followed by, "You bring nothing but shame on us! We will put you in a school for dummies, do you understand me?" Hearing those words as a 13-year-old girl created a flashback to my 8-year-old self. On that night I had sat up in bed with a knot in my stomach and said, "I have something to say!"

But my childhood laid the foundation for a life of fear, suppressing my feelings, accepting the chaos of abuse, and learning not to trust others. For many years the mental and emotional abuse inflicted by many people had blocked my ability to stand up for myself or to even be myself. It was many years later that I gathered my Self (my ideas, my feelings, my desires for life) and rebooted my thinking in a way that allowed me to escape the abuse that had haunted me all my life.

I always knew that there are many others like me who are victims of cruel people. Sometimes these abusers are significant others, and sometimes parents. They could also be bullying classmates, bosses, adult children, and sexual abusers. And some abusers assume all of these roles.

One day a light bulb went on in my head: the realization came to me that I had rebooted both my thinking and my sad, repressed, intimidated soul to the point that I had real pride in myself, that I had escaped the mental and emotional clutter that had kept me from seeing my way to a better future, and that I had indeed rebooted my life.

That was the day I knew that the right thing to do was to write down the steps that had taken me to a life that was new to me. It is a life where I decide for myself what to do, not only for today, but for my whole future. It is a life that I had seen others living but never thought I could live myself.

MY STORY – IT STARTED WHEN MY PARENTS WERE CHILDREN

Born in the Netherlands, I was raised in the small town of Voorburg, near The Hague. In earlier times it had been inside a Roman fort, but at the time its only claim to fame was a tiny museum with some Roman coins on display in dusty showcases.

When I was very little, Voorburg was a quiet and lovely little place. It had a Main Street with lots of little shops and a blacksmith. I remember walking down that street with my mother and stopping to watch huge horses being shod. They were used to pull just about everything from small carts to huge delivery vans. During the German occupation a few years later that street played a major role in my young life.

My parents were high school sweethearts and had met while ice–skating with local children. My grandfather on my father's side was the director of an Institute for Juvenile Delinquents and, as was the custom in those days, he did not spare the rod either at the institute or at home. My father and his sister grew up with this physical abuse, and it was no wonder that he left home soon after high school.

My father (to this day, I don't refer to him as "Dad") decided to go out into the world and make his fortune in Indonesia working for a large Dutch oil company. He made good money and could afford a large house with servants, a peacock, and a tethered alligator! After a year he sent for my mother who, as was the custom in those days, had married him in the Netherlands with her father as a stand-in. It wouldn't do to have an unmarried woman sail alone! Upon arrival in the Orient she settled into a far different life than she had ever known.

Earlier in my mother's life, when she was twelve years old, she had experienced a traumatic and pivotal event. Her parents divorced – not a common occurrence at that time – and her mother decided to start "fresh." She must have been very strong because she physically picked up her daughter and thrust her into her father's arms. Without a parting word, my grandmother turned and walked out of my mother's life forever.

As a result my mother became a very needy person. She craved love and attention and depended upon my father for everything. Try as she might, she was not happy living in Indonesia. My father buried himself in his work, giving no time to the wife he had dropped into an alien environment. She was left with very little to do. After several unhappy years, her health became an issue and they returned to the Netherlands where my father started anew as a tax consultant for the local farmers. Again he buried himself in his work and again my mother was left by herself, until she finally conceived at age forty, and I came along.

Because I didn't see my father much, my early years were happy ones. My mother lavished all her attention on me. I remember trips to the beach and donkey rides, kisses and bedtime stories!

One day, when I was five years old, I woke up from my afternoon nap, startled by a strange droning sound. I stood up in bed, peered out the window and saw that the sky was covered with little men hanging from funny balloons. I called, "Mom! What is that sound? What are those balloons?" No answer.

I wasn't scared, but I slipped out of bed and ran downstairs calling, "Mom! Mom! Where are you?" Just then there was an awful sound! Now I was frightened. Screaming, I ran outside, and there were my parents and all the neighbors, standing around, fear on their faces, talking in hushed voices.

Everyone stopped talking. I clutched my mother's arm and sobbed, "Mom, what is that noise? Why are the balloons in the sky?"

She gently but firmly took me back inside and explained that that noise was a siren and that I would hear a lot of that noise but I needn't be frightened. The balloons? Why, the men were just practicing jumping out of airplanes!

That was the beginning of my war experience which would culminate three years later in a fear so great it still hounds me to this day. Over the next few years the war slowly got worse, but as a child I didn't pay much attention.

Not far from where we lived were meadows sprinkled with buttercups. I loved to go and pluck them! I would pick as many as my little hand could hold. Of course there were plenty of cows, too. Absorbed as I was in the flowers, there was many a time I didn't look where I was going and splat, I either fell down in the wrong place or my sandals were sopping.

I came home reeking of manure and my mother sat me down on a kitchen chair and carefully, her hands wrapped in an old towel, untied the sandals and dropped them in the sink. She loved the buttercups and always put them on the dining table, where they floated in a big bowl, sunny yellow heads peaking over the edge.

My mother and I were close then. We often used to go biking together, me strapped securely in a little carrier on the back. We always stopped for an ice cream for me and a cup of tea for her. In the fall we would walk to a nearby park where there were several trees that dropped small nut-like clusters. My mother and I gathered a pail full and, once home, she sprinkled them with sugar and baked them in the oven.

"Are they done yet, Mom?"

"Soon, dear. Why don't you get some plates?"

Then we sat at the kitchen table munching on our "snacks."

Those were the happiest memories of my life!

However, because I had come so late in her life, my mother was, naturally, very protective. She sheltered me from everything. If I lost a game of marbles and was crying, she would go to the parents of the other girl and ask for the marbles back. In the second grade there was a competition to see who could grow the best zinnias. My mother took over the project and of course I (she) won. The word spread, and my life became miserable. In addition, Mom's passion was making clothes for me, and oh, how I hated that! In school bullying and teasing were the norm. My classmates loved to make fun of the shy, naïve little girl in homemade clothes! I painfully remember a crocheted yellow top with blue crocheted flowers sewn on. I never let on, though, how bad I felt, and I suppressed my feelings – maybe because I knew my mother was all I had. Fear ruled my life, and it was fortunate no one could see the big knot in my stomach when I had to go to school.

The situation at home had also deteriorated. My father had an office on the second floor of our house and strict rules were laid down. "No singing, whistling, or making loud noises. I get distracted and then I can't work." My mother was so cowed by my father's presence that she immediately agreed to anything he said. And so the house became quiet as a tomb. I became so afraid of making a noise and having to face the wrath of my father that I just crept quietly up the stairs to my bedroom and came down only at mealtime. It has taken me years to overcome my fear of authority.

However, the situation wasn't all bleak. I had one girlfriend, Anne, who lived a block away. She had wonderful, caring parents, and every day I went over to her house. We played, sang, and were allowed to make all the noise we wanted. Her parents even listened to us! That house became my safety net, and I have always considered her parents as my own. In fact, when they were still alive, I visited them whenever I was in Holland, sent cards, and kept in touch with them. Anne and I have remained close friends, and when I am back in the old country, we pick up where we left off!

The war intensified. As time went by, I became much more aware of what was going on. One day I noticed some people wearing yellow stars on their clothing.

"Why is that, Mom?"

"These people have to wear the stars on their clothing. The Germans gave this order. Now please, don't ask so many questions."

I learned not to ask. My "whys" never got answered. My desire to learn was unimportant.

On the other side of the park in front of our house was my elementary school. It had a big siren on top which I could see from my bedroom window. It looked like a big, ugly, black mushroom. Often, it blared its warning at night and woke me up. I would put the blankets over my head, wishing it would stop! In time, however, I learned to live with shrieking sirens.

One day the war became a true part of my life. Returning from school I noticed unusual activity going on in our neighborhood. Bulldozers were lined up and there were a lot of serious-looking men. The pretty tree-lined little park had had lots of benches where one could enjoy the many colorful flowers. Now the local militia was converting this peaceful place into an underground bomb shelter. Gone were the beautiful trees and rose bushes. Instead, there was a half-oval bunker of cement that was covered with sod so grass could grow over it as a camouflage. The entrance faced the front of our house and we could see a ramp that descended slowly into the gaping darkness. The bravest of us children ventured into that hole and ran back, excitedly telling the rest of the kids that there were benches on each side and there was no way out except through the front!

Naturally, my most vivid memories are of the time towards the end of the war when I was a little older.

One evening the school siren shrieked again. By this time we were used to its sound and the rumbling noise of approaching bombs. They were bound for London, England. The roaring sound of these V-1 and V-2 bombs hurtling overhead was nothing new. But this time it was different. This bomb exploded with a horrendous BOOM into a smoking fireball, causing major damage in a populated area not too far from us. Houses were blown to bits, people killed, and fires everywhere. That night there was a stiff wind blowing in from the North Sea. It stoked the flames and propelled smoke and little charred pieces of another town's lives, and they rained down on our street and home. Fear then took a firm grip. What if we were next?

The most terrifying experience of my life occurred when I was eight years old. It was spring, the most colorful time in the Netherlands. Tulips and daffodils were everywhere, the trees were budding, and shrubs were covered with tiny pink flowers. In contrast, the war had grown worse and fighting was everywhere, but there was still a certain measure of freedom as long as a person had an ID.

After dinner one pleasant evening, my mother and I took a walk to Main Street. I loved going there because it meant we passed the train station and I could watch the trains rumble by. We set off for a 20-minute walk, and I skipped ahead, full of excitement. Leaving the quiet house was a treat for me, and having my mother with me made the outing twice as exciting!

We sat at the station for a few minutes, playing a guessing game as to where the trains were coming from (they were always headed for The Hague), and then walked down to Main Street. We were halfway down the street when we spotted a large mass of people coming toward us, walking in the street! On the sidewalks, on each side, were German soldiers with their rifles at the ready, poking and prodding the group along. Before we knew what was happening we were swept up in this tide of humanity, turning back towards the station!

I was frightened, but at first not unduly so. I was with my mother, right? I clutched her arm, asking, "Mom, what's going on? Where're we going?"

"Til, you have to be quiet and hold on tight. I don't know yet where we are going."

Her voice was a little different, anxious – and this set off an alarm.

"Mom, you do have your ID, don't you?" If she did, everything would be fine and I wouldn't have to worry. To my shock she answered, "No, Til, I left it on the kitchen table." On the kitchen table? What would happen now? Without an ID we would be at the mercy of the Germans, I knew that for sure. The radio had often warned people not to go out without their ID.

I lost it completely. I tugged at the arm of the man next to me, looked up at him, and screamed, "We don't have an ID!" I can only imagine the chill this must have sent through my mother. The man mumbled something, shrugged himself free of me, and shuffled on.

My mother then gripped me firmly and said, "Til, do not scream. You are not helping at all!" I sobbed and sobbed, but I buried my desire to scream. In retrospect it was not a very smart thing for my mother to tell me that we didn't have an ID, but the damage was done.

We moved along with the group, three soldiers on each side. Finally we saw the station again, but there was a turn in the road just before the building. A few of the soldiers went ahead to block the oncoming traffic, and that's when my mother saw her chance.

Slowly, very slowly she pushed to the side of the road. When there was no immediate control in sight, she slipped under the overhang of a house on the corner, out of sight, dragging me with her. From there we walked into a side street, where we and the Germans still could catch sight of each other. At any moment I expected to be ordered to turn around or to be shot. The hair on the back of my neck was standing on end, but nothing happened. Walking silently side by side we took the long way home.

That event made me lose trust in my mother. How could she forget her ID? Later I learned that the station was used as a holding facility. Germany needed manpower to work in their factories and anyone without an ID was fair game. My mother had had the courage and presence of mind to put her life on the line by escaping, but of course that was just one of the things I didn't realize until much later. At that moment I was a scared young girl who was told by her parents that everything had turned out fine – why was I making such a fuss?

So it kept being re-confirmed to me that I should suppress my feelings, my thoughts, and my Self, and pretend that everything was all right.

A second pivotal episode during the war years occurred toward the end of the war. Germany had lost many troops and increasingly older men (those above age 40) were taken and forced to work in factories. One day my mother and I were eating lunch while my father was out, when all of a sudden there was a tremendous pounding on the door. My mother was not quick enough to open it so it was broken down, and in stormed three soldiers. We were ordered to stand against the wall while one of them guarded us. The other two searched the house from top to bottom, looking for my father.

They went up to the attic where my mother had hoarded some food. Food was extremely scarce, but my father did tax work for farmers who shared some extra produce with him when there was something to spare. We heard the soldiers coming down and saw them leave, without so much as a glance in our direction. My mother's eagle eye, however, detected them munching on our apples, and if looks could have killed, it would have been the end of them.

Fear, always fear. How dare they come into our home and steal our apples!

Being an only child, I was lucky that I always had something to eat. Whatever there was – an old potato, a smidgen of meat – was given to my father and me. My mother simply did without. Much later I learned she lost more than 90 pounds by the time the war ended!

The winter of 1944-45 was horrific and became known as the Hunger Winter because there was little left to eat, although the black market flourished! People who had nothing more to sell ate tulip bulbs and potato peels, and scrounged around for little pieces of coal to keep warm. The only heat we had came from a tiny round can which fitted on top of our regular stove. You could put twigs in there, a little piece of coal, and some pieces of wood if you were lucky. This little can warmed part of our living room but you had to sit close to it. My father had always been able to rustle up a tiny bit of this and that which he hid under his coat as he biked home and had to pass several German inspections. Now this too had become impossible.

In an effort to find more, my father decided to bike to the northern part of Holland where the fighting was less intense and maybe, just maybe, he would come home with something. It was a two-day trek. The tires on his bike were long gone so he set off on his bike with just the rims. I can still see my mother, looking in the mirror, straightening her yellow blouse and turning to me with a brave smile after he left. What must have gone through her mind? Would she ever see my father again? He did make it though.

Within a week he was back, totally exhausted. He had been given a sack of corn which he had held with one hand on the handlebars while steering with the other. His hands shook for days! Also, I have never understood how he managed to evade the German control posts; he never spoke about it.

Dutch people don't eat corn as a rule – they give it to the pigs – but were we glad to have it! We ate corn every day, but in moderation, because it had to last. My father would go to work on his old bike, and on its back carrier he would have a small bowl of boiled corn, carefully wrapped in a red handkerchief and securely fastened. Sometimes it was mixed with some boiled tulips for variety!

By the end of the war, fear and lack of trust had firmly embedded itself into my psyche. My mother, upon whom I had always relied, now would not answer any questions whatsoever and I was terribly lonely.

At long last, on May 5, 1945, a voice on the radio announced that the war had finally ended. Again the neighbors poured out of their homes.

"Did you hear it? Germany has surrendered!" Flags were flying and our national anthem was played over and over again. What a day!

For me, however, God had a special sign that the war was over. A few weeks later I was on my way to my girlfriend's house. It was a beautiful spring day with clear blue skies and I again heard a droning sound. Looking up, I saw a silver airplane with a large Red Cross sign painted on its side. Later I learned that it was a Swedish plane carrying food for us. It was slowly and carefully descending but released its load too soon. The container fell to the ground and burst open unexpectedly in the street. For one brief shining moment I was alone in the street with a broken chocolate bar at my feet. Then, of course, everyone ran out and scooped up whatever they could.

Now my war was really over and life returned more or less to normal.

The other side of the coin, however, was that at home the situation had worsened. I was ignored most of the time by my father, and my mother, though still concerned about me, had withdrawn. I just couldn't figure out why. Time and again I asked her what was the matter, and always the answer was, "Nothing, nothing at all."

When I was nine, I had a revelation. I know it sounds strange. As usual I had spent some time at Anne's house, where I was allowed to be myself. There must have been a birthday or other celebration because I remember cake, lemonade, and lots of singing. The Dutch are great on birthdays!

Then, when it was time to go home, an old familiar feeling started, a knot in my stomach and fear. Fear I would meet my father. That night I sat up in bed and for the first time consciously realized that something was wrong. Why was I always so happy to leave the house and so down when it was time to go home? I just knew something was wrong.

I started to compare Anne's parents with mine. How caring and loving they were. Anne's father had even made me a small doll's cradle once, just because. I said out loud, "I want parents like Anne has, and I want people to listen to me because I have something to say!"

What it was I wanted to say, I don't know, but that little vision has culminated years and years later in my becoming an inspirational speaker on abuse, fear, and relationships.

When I was a sophomore in high school, my mother had a terrible accident, a pivotal event in both our lives. After that she joined my father in emotionally and mentally abusing me.

It was winter and coal was still scarce, so we barely heated our living room. Of course the kitchen, bedroom, and bathroom were ice cold, but I was used to that. My father's office was another matter. He had three people working for him there during the day, and they needed heat. My parents had managed to scrounge together some coal that was kept in a shed in our back yard. It was almost exclusively used for the office. During the day it was the task of our help to lug two coal buckets up the winding narrow Dutch stairs and pour a bucketful into the gaping opening of an old-fashioned coal stove.

It was my father's habit to read the paper after dinner, then go upstairs to work until 10:00 o'clock when he would go to bed. This meant the office had to be kept warm, and it was my mother's task to get another bucket full of coal, bring it upstairs, and "feed" the stove.

I still see her looking at her watch, saying, "It's time," wrapping herself warmly against the fierce cold, walking through the kitchen, and going outside. I heard the usual sounds – the coal rattling into the bucket, the outside door clanging shut, and my mother's dragging footsteps through the kitchen, down the hall, and up the stairs.

All of a sudden there was an awful scream! We rushed out into the hall and found her lying on the floor, legs bent at angles. She was covered in coal and dust, and was so pale! She was moaning.

My father called an ambulance and he went with her to the hospital, but not without telling me to clean up the mess and go to bed because there was school tomorrow. As if I could sleep!

Hours and hours went by without a message. I sat in the living room, listening to the ticktock of the grandfather's clock. One o'clock, two o'clock. I was so fearful that I started to pray, "Please God, make her well and let her come home soon. She is all I have…" Until finally I heard the key turn in the lock.

"How is Mom?" I asked.

"She has shattered both her knee caps and it is doubtful she will ever walk again" was the answer. Then, "Why aren't you in bed like I told you to?"

I was numb.

My mother was in the hospital for six weeks and I couldn't wait for her to get home.

My father hired a housekeeper from the Red Cross. She cooked, cleaned some, and then left. We ate in silence – my father in his big chair at the head of the table, I sitting in my accustomed place to the side. He drank his glass of water, then got up, and headed back to his office till 10:00 pm. I went to my room to do homework and read. Fortunately I was a voracious reader at that time, escaping to fun and interesting places, often finishing a couple of books a week.

Voorburg didn't have a hospital, so my mother was in a hospital about twelve miles away. I tried to visit her as often as I could. I took my bike and some schoolwork and sat next to her bed. She didn't say much and slept a lot, but at least I felt there was some connection.

Finally the day came when she was released. I was at school when she came home but oh, was I glad to see her! Now everything would be back to normal!

But it wasn't and never would be again. The mother I had had before was kind and loving, though somewhat remote. Now she was a different person. She had become a bitter woman, turned inward, who lashed out at her family and the world. Her crutches were always near her. She would try to hobble about, but her balance was off and she was very prone to falling.

Today I realize that when she found out that she would be a cripple forever, her personality changed. She was full of anger.

Exercises were prescribed, but my father convinced her not to try. It would exhaust her too much; it would cause too much pain. She would be much better off staying off her feet, and he would take care of her. Because she was so influenced by my father, she took his word as the gospel and gave up trying.

I was lost, and suppressed again all feelings of fear and anger. Having a knot in my stomach was a constant state and, I too, became depressed. Anne and her parents did what they could to help and support me, but my schoolwork began to suffer and pretty soon I knew I was failing. At that time it was customary that final report cards were sent home by mail, and for days I paced up and down in the hallway, waiting for the mail to arrive.

Then one day, there it was, the dreaded envelope! Of course I was not home when it came, and when I saw the pile of mail on the dining room table, I knew the worst was about to happen. My father had a terrible temper that I had been on the receiving end of many times when there was an infraction of his rules!

He picked up the envelope, slid out the report card, looked at it, and then turned around, red-faced and with bulging eyes.

"How dare you, you stupid girl!" he screamed. "All Fs! Don't you have any brains?" More choice words. Then, "You bring nothing but shame on us! We will put you in a school for dummies, do you understand me?"

My mother took his part. "Til, how could you? Don't you know that you shame us, having a daughter who fails? I knew that compared to Anne, you were not very bright, but this, this is beyond words."

On and on it went. I just let the abuse run over me. Although my fear and hopelessness increased by the minute, I worked to I suppress my feelings so I could reach the point of being numb.

I was enrolled the next year in an upscale all-girls school in The Hague. Most of girls came from well-to-do families, of course, and they were not particularly interested in this quiet, withdrawn girl who came from another town. But I didn't mind being left alone because it was better than being subjected to bullying like I had been before. I discovered that I had a flair for languages and did well, but it seemed I could not please my mother. "You know the school you are in now is for dummies, don't you?" and "Why don't you ever go to see your father upstairs? You know he loves you." Maybe so, in his way, but I wasn't about to see how.

The years passed. I was a senior in high school. I didn't see Anne much anymore because she had gone to a different school and had other friends. I simply plodded on. Up at six, eat breakfast, make my lunch, and head off to school on my bike. My mother stayed in bed till ten. My father was up at six, too, but mercifully was in his office.

There is no school transportation in Holland; students have to make their own way. Rain or shine I peddled for a good hour against the wind in the mornings to get all the way to the school in The Hague. I was always thankful in the afternoon when I had the wind at my back.

One afternoon, I was able to shave about 15 minutes from my biking time and came home early. I had just rounded the corner of our street when I noticed that there was a taxi standing in front of our house.

"How strange," I thought. "My father always uses his bike and my mother is always at home."

I wheeled my bike through the gate and was just about to open the front door when my mother appeared, fully dressed with coat and hat on, hanging on her crutches. Without a word she passed by me, followed by my father who carried a small suitcase. I just stood there, not believing what I had just seen! My mother got into the taxi, my father handed the suitcase to the driver, and off she went, without a word.

I mustered my courage. "Where did Mom go?"

I got a blast! "Your mother has left because she could no longer cope with a teenager. I told you that you make too much noise and ask too many questions of her. I've told you time and again she needs her rest. It's all your fault! God knows when she will come back." And with that he stormed up the stairs to his office and slammed the door shut.

I sat at the bottom of the stairs. "What have I done? My mother has left because of me!"

I went to my room and for the first time I bit so hard on the side of my fingers that the blood ran. I began to tear at the wounds, over and over again.

And I didn't feel a thing! Finally sanity took over and I bandaged them the best I could.

That night I decided that I would avoid my father at all costs.

Again, a housekeeper came. I ate in my room and relaxed only when I knew he was away. If I saw him coming when I was outside, I hid in the bushes until he had gone up to his office.

A couple of weeks passed without a word. Then, all of a sudden, there she was again, sitting in her chair as if nothing had happened.

"Mom, where have you been? Why did you leave without talking to me? How could you?" The words just tumbled out.

Her only response was, "Til, I needed to get away for a while." She offered no reason. Only later did I find out. She had had suspicions that my father was having an affair with his administrative assistant, Mrs. Van den Broek. She needed time to work things out, whether to stay or leave.

However, her way of leaving without saying one word to me affirmed yet again that I could trust no one. Consequently trust is an issue I have grappled with for most of my life. I graduated that year, just after my eighteenth birthday, with an extensive knowledge of French, German, and English, and my proficiency helped me enormously later in life.

After high school I went to work as a nanny in England, again, to escape my parents, but, oh boy, was I bad at it! I had had absolutely no training with small children. The children's mother had served in the army and brooked absolutely no nonsense. The children and I had a schedule which included a one and a half hour walk each day, rain or shine. I was very unhappy and so was she.

As a result I began to eat and eat, stuffing scones, teacakes, and cookies in my mouth till I blew up like a balloon!

I asked permission to go home and the mother immediately granted it. I took the next train and ferry back to Holland, relieved this was over, and expected that my mother would be glad to see me again after six months. I opened the door to the living room.

"Hi Mom, how are you? I'm back!"

"My God, Til, how fat your are! What have you been doing to yourself?" That was my welcome. Nothing had changed.

Then I found a job working at the United Nations office in The Hague. I loved it and still remember the thrill when our whole office was invited to hear a delegate speak! However, that job didn't last long either.

One day I was carrying some papers to the office of my boss. The door was slightly ajar. I carefully pushed it open, expecting to see him sitting behind his desk. Instead, there he was, on the floor, with his secretary! I didn't know where to look, dropped my papers on the desk, and ran out. Two days later I was fired for "gross incompetency"!

Next I answered an ad for an agent in a travel agency and was hired, based upon my language ability, but there I met with abuse again. The supervisor was a man with a clubfoot who sat at a desk in a corner of the room so he could keep tabs on all the employees. He had a sadistic streak and took pleasure in commenting out loud on all the foibles and characteristics of all of us. There was a young man who had a lot of body hair and he would say, "John, you need to shave your hands again. How long has it been?"

I was also the butt of his mean spirit. As a young woman I suffered now and then from acne. He would say, "I see you have acne again. Please put on a band aid so I don't have to look at it."

Oh, I absorbed and buried the pain again and again, and just went on working; quitting didn't even enter my mind.

I married when I was 21 years old, and we emigrated to the U.S. where job prospects were much better. We didn't want children at first because it takes time to adjust to a new culture. Parental pressure from both sides proved too much for us, however, so within two years we had two children, a boy and a girl. My mother had instilled in me that it is a wife's duty to have children, and so I felt that I had finally pleased them! Being pregnant was a joy to me. People took notice and gave me the attention I so desperately needed.

Of course, as is so often the case, I had perpetuated the pattern of abuse and married a man who was very much like my father. Jack was rather indifferent, keeping any positive feelings to himself. When he talked to me, it was often in an abusive way. His favorite saying was, "You were raised with the cows," meaning, I had no manners and was not living up to his idea of a "proper" wife.

One day Jack told me that the company was sending us back to the Netherlands. Unbeknownst to me, he had changed positions and had been working in their international department. What was more logical than that we would be sent back? We were fluent in both languages. Jack gave me the message just ten days before we were to leave. He was happy as a clam! Now he was somebody, sales manager of a local branch of the company.

I, on the other hand, felt enveloped in a black cloud. All I could think of was seeing my parents again and enduring their abuse. However, once back, I decided to make the best of it and concentrated all my energy on my two little ones.

We remained in the Netherlands for seven years, with a short stay in Switzerland in the middle. There I became pregnant with my third child. I was ecstatic, people would notice me again! Jack was not happy and buried himself in his work, as usual.

Once back in the States, he divorced me and married his secretary. It was a shock. I must have been very naïve because I didn't think this could ever happen, especially after twenty years of marriage!

A few years later I remarried to a man eleven years older than I was, an alcoholic who had been sober for about six months. Maybe I was looking for a caring father figure? Who knows? Anyway, within two years he ran off with my credit card and married a new love. During those years I learned he had a violent temper, and I was often the butt of his cruel jokes. When would I learn?

I lost trust in all men, decided it was time to take over my life, and went to college. I graduated with a M.Ed. in my mid-forties and embarked on a teaching career. In the meantime, my two eldest children had left the house. My older son had made a career in the army, and my daughter had set her sights high and married well. There was almost a ten-year difference between my elder and my younger son, who was still with me.

I buried all the anger and feelings of abandonment, resentment, and distrust deep inside and plodded through, teaching special education during the day and English as a Second Language at night. During summer break I worked as a tour director for a British company and, when money got really tight, I delivered newspapers. It was not surprising that I developed migraines and a pronounced tremor in my hands, but I didn't care. At least no one was abusing me.

Little did I know, a transformation was still to occur in my life. Fourteen years later, I met a wonderful man and we were married within a year. However, I still didn't trust him completely, and always expected him to leave. The slightest remark would give me a knot in my stomach and a flashback to earlier times. But his patience with me showed that this was the real thing!

Several years later my body did let me know that something was seriously wrong. All those years of abuse and repression finally came to the surface, and I was diagnosed with Post Traumatic Stress Disorder. Therapy did wonders. I have learned to become more assertive, to speak up, and not to dwell on the past.

It was also at this time, although my parents had died many years earlier, that I decided to find out more about them. I found some old family papers, and discovered the reason why my father was so controlling and abusive, and why my mother was so needy. With these new insights I was finally able to forgive them.

Today I speak about my life to as many people as possible. I want them, and you, to know that it is possible to reboot your thinking and reboot your life *at any age* by following the five-step process which is detailed in Chapter Two. You *can* make your own decisions, without fear of harsh judgment. You *can* live like you've seen others living, but never thought you could yourself. You *can* be free. *You can live your own life.*

Chapter Two

EXPLAINING THE 5-STEP PROCESS

Emotional and verbal abuse started during my elementary school years, and it continued throughout most of my life. Because I had suppressed my feelings for so long, I needed therapy. Afterwards I felt so free, I was ready to take on the world! I had ideas, plans that were just for me, not to please someone else. I wanted to become a speaker and a writer, one who would be able to inspire others – tell them that they *can* overcome these feelings of worthlessness and low self-esteem!

How did I get these ideas and plans? To be honest, I don't exactly know. What I did know was that I saw myself doing these things, and how wonderful that would be. But it had to be more than just picturing myself as such. I had to make a decision, would I go ahead with what I envisioned or not? At my age that wouldn't be easy! What were the drawbacks? I needed to have self-confidence, that I knew, and I needed the kind of friends who would not shoot my plans down. I would also have to be very careful not to lure myself back into thinking it was all a pipe dream.

So I developed a 5-step process. It starts with a Vision. In order to make this Vision a reality, I needed to be Committed. I needed to be Assertive and stand up for myself. I needed to be with people who would Support me so that I could remain strong in my thinking. And I definitely needed to be Vigilant, so that I would maintain my new life. These steps may vary a bit in their order as they are applied to other people's lives, but they made it possible for me to achieve my Vision for my future, and they will make it possible for you as well.

From talking with other people who had overcome different kinds of abuse, I realized that many of them had *unconsciously* achieved their vision for a better life by using the same steps I had *consciously* identified and carried out (although I didn't know I would make a process out of them at the time). So I decided to share this process with others who could benefit from it. Abuse shouldn't happen in the first place, but there is a way out!

THE 5-STEPS

Step 1: Vision – Create one for yourself.

Visions come in all shapes and sizes, so I would like to take you on an imaginary car trip. We have plenty of time so I will ask you to let your thoughts roam free. Where have you always wanted to go? Maybe it is the California coast with its barking sea lions, or the mesas in the West. Maybe you like the wide-open fields in the Midwest or the mountains, or you might just see something you like around the corner, in which case it would be a very short car ride! But I know *something* will strike you and you will say, "Yes, that's it. That's where I want to be." And you can see yourself in that place.

That is having a vision. You feel so strongly about that place that you would be willing to work hard to make the trip there.

Now, let's move our thoughts in another direction. Is there something you have always wanted to do but never dared to? A friend of mine always wanted to go to India but never had the courage. One summer, when she was in her thirties, she had a vision of herself visiting the Taj Mahal. It was so strong that she left her two children with her mother for two months, and off she went. It was the best experience of her life, she said. It made her more self-reliant and self-assured, and it made her a better teacher.

Now bring it closer to home. Are you living in an abusive relationship? Do you have a vision of creating a new life for yourself? How would you feel if you actually made your vision a reality? The quality of your life would improve tremendously and you would come to realize that no one – not you or anyone else – should have to endure abuse, ever.

Step 2: Commitment – It will make your future.

Now that you have decided on a vision, it's time to make a commitment. The road to achieving a vision is rarely straight; you will have to deal with twists and turns and up and downs. Making a commitment to a vision also means that you will have to step outside your comfort zone, which might make you *uncomfortable.* There will be moments that you will say to yourself, "Enough already, I'm going back to my old familiar way of thinking."

The way to deal with this is to set up a time line. Divide the path to reach your vision into small reasonable accomplishments. For instance, if you wanted to get out of an abusive relationship, what would you do first? Take a couple of days to think things through. Ask yourself if you would be better off postponing leaving your abuser till you have made a plan, or are you ready to leave right now? It all depends on your situation.

Okay, you have decided to make a plan first. And for the next few weeks you are committed to getting some things together. The first thing you need to do is get a good-sized bag. CASA (Community Action Stops Abuse) is a St. Petersburg, Florida, shelter for abused women. It has an extensive checklist you might want to consult, but here are some of the items you could consider putting into it:

- ☐ Identification
- ☐ Birth Certificates
- ☐ Social Security cards
- ☐ Extra cash
- ☐ Bank books
- ☐ Insurance papers
- ☐ Extra house and car keys
- ☐ Medications
- ☐ Pictures of family members (including the abuser)
- ☐ School and college records

☐   Copy of Injunction for Protection
(if you have one)

Check these off as you go along.

Now that these are in the bag, so to speak, consider opening a separate bank account in your own name, and have the statement sent to a post office box or to a friend's or relative's address. You would have to keep account and PIN number secret. Do you have trusted friends you can count on to help you? Do they have friends in turn who would be willing to put you up for a couple of weeks if you had to find a new job? Can you or will you need to get a restraining order? What about your car? Are you a two-car or a one-car family – or is one car in your name? Can you find other transportation if you only have one car? If you have children, how would you take them with you? Pick them up from daycare or school? What do you tell the principal when you withdraw them? Where would you go? You may want to contact a local abuse shelter for more specific guidance.

If you have no resources, is there a shelter for abused women in your area or in the town you want to move to? If so, get its number and make inquiries. Is there room for you and your children, or is there a waiting list? How long do they offer refuge for? Are you working outside the home? You may have to quit your job if you do not want your abuser find you. That will be one of the hardest decisions to make. If you are moving to another town in another state, you will have to do some research and look for a job there before you leave. You may have to take what's available at first, but you will need an income. These are some of the questions and decisions you will have to face in the next few months.

Of course, if you are in an abusive relationship and your vision is to leave very soon, you need to make sure you have found temporary shelter where you can safely make up your mind where you want to go and what you would like your future to be.

Step 3: Assertiveness – Stand up for yourself.

Standing up for yourself does not mean being aggressive. People often make that mistake. Assertiveness simply means that you will develop the courage to say, "I have made the commitment for a better life" and mean it. As a friend likes to say, "I can stay under the bed and peek out now and then, or I can crawl out from under and face the world squarely."

You have decided to go outside your comfort zone, and make a new future. Good for you! Now is the time to put your plan into action. Open that bank account. Go to the library and read the want ads in the papers of the new town you have chosen. If you have older children, now *may* be the time to take them aside and explain that no person should have to live with disrespect and verbal abuse and that you hope they will never become abusers. If you are sure they can keep from talking about it, tell them that your mind is made up to leave and what you plan to do. Think about what parts of the plan (like your bank account, timing, or destination) you don't need to share with them. Be frank but firm. This is your life you are talking about.

Children are very resilient, although they may be scared at first, but you are in charge now and you can reassure them that you will look out for their best interests. If your children are juniors or seniors in high school, one of them may opt to stay with your husband (if he isn't abusive to them). You will have to take a deep breath and let him or her go. You have to do what's best for you.

At this stage in your plan of escape you need to check and double check. Do you have a private account set up, a post office box, maybe some clothes stashed away? Do you have money, or did you take money out of your account? Is there someone in the area you want to go to who stands at the ready to receive you and your children? Has your husband become suspicious? Has he varied his routine to check up on you?

Check what could possibly go wrong, and have a Plan B. Be sure the friends who will help you know of this plan. You probably are nervous and you will need to know that they are able to accommodate you should there be a change of date or hour. Whatever you do, do not postpone things for so long that you decide not to escape. Then, at exactly the right moment, you take whatever you've decided on, step out of the house, and do not look back. Your new life is waiting!

Step 4: Support System – Surround yourself with positive people.

You do not want to hang out with people who are negative thinkers. It is so easy to crawl back under the bed again when you hear, "Why on earth would you want to do that? You know there are some good things about your partner (abuser), too." Or, "Things aren't as bad as you say they are. Your partner is a perfectly nice man." You get the picture. It might even become necessary to drop some old friends, painful as that may be.

But consider this: Are you willing to give up your vision, commitment, and assertiveness now that you have come far enough to give serious thought to having a better future? No; far better to cultivate a new circle of friends, ones who are positive and will cheer you on! They know you are not perfect, that you will have doubts and fears, but they urge you on to keep trying. Every step you take scaling the mountain is one in the right direction.

Step 5: Vigilance – Maintain your strength and your safety.

The dictionary says vigilance means being continually on the alert and remaining watchful for any sign of trouble. That doesn't mean you have to continually look over your shoulder, but you may need to stay in touch with trusted friends who can keep you informed about what's going on.

Is your former abuser making plans to find you? If you were married, is he planning to divorce you? Are you planning to divorce him? It also means you have some emotional healing to do. Visit a library and find books, poems, or articles that speak to your feelings. Realize you have every reason to be proud of yourself. That alone is enough to give you a sense of power!

Find out if there are support groups for abused women in your area. They do provide great support and you can learn from people who've walked in your shoes what mistakes not to make.

Inform the principal of the new schools your children are enrolled in of your situation. Instruct them never to reveal the fact that they are attending or to give out their home address to anyone who is not on your "to be trusted" list. Above all, have faith in yourself that you did the right thing! You are a caring, wonderful person!

CONCLUSION

In conclusion, these five steps

- Vision
- Commitment
- Assertiveness
- Positive Support
- Vigilance

have been used, not necessarily in that order, by the people in this book who have experienced various forms of emotional, verbal, and sexual abuse.

In the following chapters I will tell the stories of these people. I thank them profoundly for their courage and the inspiration they gave me. They were willing to come forward and relate to me how, by using the 5 steps, they made better lives for themselves. Of course their names have been changed to protect their identities.

Chapter Three

ABUSE BY A SPOUSE OR A SIGNIFICANT OTHER

Although in this chapter I have concentrated on spouse abuse or abuse by a male, plenty of it is perpetrated by females on their male partners, but fewer statistics have been documented on this than on the more common male-on-female abuse.

Statistics show that 29% of all women have been subjected to physical abuse. What a huge percentage! Even higher is the percentage of women who have experienced emotional and verbal abuse! Emotional abuse, like physical abuse, is used to control, demean, or punish a woman.

Like other kinds of abuse, this one is not limited to one or two sociological groups. Rich, poor, black, white, yellow, educated, professional or not – it can show up in just about any household. Quite often the abuser can deceive the outside world with his charm so no one suspects what is really going on behind closed doors. The victim often does not reveal the truth for fear of retaliation.

Here is a list of classic characteristics of an abuser. Let me state, however, that not every woman experiences all of them.

1. **Presses for commitment early** in the relationship. "Why wait? We've been dating for a while. Let's surprise everyone with an engagement announcement. You'd like that, wouldn't you?" Or: "Tell me you love me."

2. **Is critical of many things,** including your appearance, sexual performance, opinions, ability as a parent, job performance, other abilities or shortcomings (real or imagined). He may call the woman stupid, fat, ugly, or worse. "Who would want you? Just look at yourself!" Or: "Do you remember so and so? Now SHE was a looker, slim and so attractive! I wouldn't mind being married to HER!" For many years I lived with the following: "You were raised with the cows. You have no manners." "You may be a good mother but you are not a good wife." "You have such broad shoulders, you can carry anything." (Just load the abuse on.) "I will say you can cook but you are only a

short order cook." "Why can't you cook a turkey like everyone else?" (This after having just arrived from the Netherlands where they didn't cook turkeys!)

A report by Women's Aid, a charity dedicated to ending domestic abuse, found that disabled women experience domestic abuse over a longer period and suffer more severe injuries than those who aren't disabled. A caretaker or personal assistant may also be an abuser. He or she may withhold care, remove mobility or sensory devices, or use the woman's disability to taunt or degrade her. Family and friends may find it difficult to believe the victim; after all, who would abuse a disabled woman?

3. **Demeans you** by refusing to a) listen to your opinions; b) listen to logic, criticism, or input from you; c) let you finish a sentence. The abuser is superior to you and knows better than you. So why listen to you? 4) have your children treat you with respect. "Don't listen to mommy. You do what I tell you." Or, "When I come back

tonight, I want you to tell me what mommy has done, or else."

4. **Demands control** of time, money, physical environment, whether you have a job and which one, and more. An abuser controls the money, what is spent and how it is spent, not allowing access to the money, or conversely, he does not contribute to any of the household expenses. He forbids you to work, or if he does let you work, he requires that you give your paycheck to him. He forbids you to have money of your own unless it is for a specific purpose, and then detailed documentation is required after the purchase.

5. **Has a quick temper** and overreacts to minor things. The least little thing can set him off. A friend of mine told me she had given away a seldom-used Christmas ornament to a charity. She made the mistake of telling her husband and he immediately blew up. Why hadn't she discussed it with him? "You know I will decide when and what we will donate!"

6. **Makes threats to** a) hurt or kill you or your children, b) take or destroy your belongings, including your keys, car, and important papers, c) hurt of kill himself. And more. He knows you don't have any money and so you would have to come to him with your hand held out. Or: "I will kill myself if your leave. Do you want to have that on your conscience?" "You know I love you, so why would you want to leave?" He is playing on your emotions.

7. **Isolates you** from your family, your friends, and what you want to do. In the beginning of a relationship, it may seem like an expression of love or concern. As time passes, jealousy turns to entitlement and possessiveness. Because of your limited contact with the outside world, you may not be aware of community resources that will give you support.

8. **Makes all the rules** and demands that you follow them, including unreasonable demands and unwanted sexual demands. He wants to have children soon. He undermines

your value and authority in front of your children. (See # 3).

9. **Is physically abusive** by a) attacking you with his body or objects, b) abandoning you, c) locking you out, d) treating you as property or a sex object, e) hurting you when you are sick or pregnant. And more.

10. **Makes you feel trapped** in the relationship. An abuser prevents you from having independent activities, going to classes, or simply belonging to a club. He may falsely accuse you of having a relationship or push you into having sex to prove your love. The abuser feels he should be the one and only focus of your life.

11. In public, **is either very charming or humiliates you** in front of others. For instance, you are at a dinner party where the hostess has set a beautiful table. The abuser looks your way and says, "You should get so-and-so to teach you how to set a table like this."

12. **Uses a sincere tone** to get what he wants. He makes promises, you get your hopes up, and nothing happens. He lies.

13. **Has a history** of being abused as a child. This should raise a red flag! Consider your options carefully. It may lead to abuse for you and/or your children. Take it slow, don't rush into anything, and get to know him on a deeper level. Maybe even suggest pre-marital counseling.

14. **Blames you for the abuse and for everything else!**

If you recognize someone in your life who has some of these characteristics, stop and think. This person could be toxic to you. That means poisonous. It could mean he is trying to take away your value as a person. You need to be aware that everyone has the right to have opinions that differ from others and that everyone is to be treated with respect. **Including you.**

The following stories are about courageous women who, by rebooting their thinking, rebooted their lives using the 5 steps I have identified, even though they may not have known it at that time. The 5 steps work because they make sense.

Betty

Betty lived in California, was married for several years, and had two small children. Her husband Hal was a typical abuser. He checked up on her constantly by phone and came home at different times to make sure she was there. If she wasn't, she would have to have a good explanation.

Hal was very jealous. He forbade Betty to have friends, but she displayed her first bit of assertiveness by having a good friend, Julia, without Hal's knowledge. Julia was the support Betty needed. They met in secret on street corners or at the park and talked for a few minutes when it was possible.

Hal was well-known and well liked in the community and made excellent money, but at home he was a different person. He did all the shopping and accompanied Betty and her daughters to the store whenever they needed new clothes.

Finally, life became intolerable for Betty. By rebooting her thinking she formulated a vision of life without constant fear. She devised a plan of escape and made a conscious commitment to it. Little by little she put a few clothes for herself and her daughters in an old duffel bag and hid it in the back of the closet. Months passed. She also managed to squirrel away a few dollars here and there and put those in an envelope stashed in the suitcase.

Meanwhile Betty secretly continued to meet with Julia. They discussed how to get her and her children out without Hal's finding out. She wanted to go as far away as possible – ideally to Europe, but the cost was prohibitive. So she settled on Florida. Finally they chose a date and time. There was going to be only a half hour between Hal's going to work and arriving there before he would check on her again.

The day of Betty's ultimate assertiveness arrived. She took the duffel bag from the back of the closet and left the house with just the clothes on her back and $25 in cash. Julia was waiting in a car on the corner, so that she couldn't be traced. The two women drove to the daycare and picked up the girls on the pretext that their grandma had taken ill and they were going to visit her. They headed straight to the airport and had just enough time for Betty and her girls to make a flight to Chicago. Julia had a friend there who met them at the airport and drove them all to Florida.

Julia wired her money so she was able to rent a small apartment. Betty also rented a post office box and used that as her address so that she would be more difficult to find. Then she put her two little ones in a church daycare facility and started looking for a job.

At first Betty started cleaning houses. The money wasn't great, but she put as much aside as possible and was able to pay the people back who had helped her. Betty was amazed at her successes. They gave her the courage to set even more goals for herself. She had rebooted her life successfully. With help from some people in her church she was able to start her own cleaning agency. It's been a long time, but to this day she is still vigilant. She fights off the inclination to go back to her old thinking habits and keeps an eye out in case her husband shows up.

This is what can happen when a woman has a Vision of freedom from abuse, makes a Commitment to it, musters up her Assertiveness, finds a Support System, and is Vigilant about her strength and her safety. Don't you just love it when a plan comes together?

Veronica

Veronica and her husband Ralph had no children and lived in a rural community where neighbors were miles away from each other. The nearest grocery store was fifty miles away. To say that she was isolated would be an understatement.

They boarded horses and Veronica had one of her own, a roan named Precious. She loved to go riding, especially early in the morning when the sun was barely above the mountains. She lavished all her devotion on Precious, who seemed to understand her mistress's anxiety and fears. Veronica also had two dogs that roamed the countryside at will but were always there in the evening for their meal.

Ralph was a person not to be trifled with, and woe be unto the person who dared to argue with him. Muscled and macho, his passions were bodybuilding and hunting. His bedroom was filled with exercise equipment, and the walls were covered with bows and arrows and rifles. He was a crack shot.

Ralph was in charge of their business, did all the shopping, and paid the bills. He was known for his temper but could charm the birds out of the trees when someone brought a new horse to be boarded. He often yelled at Veronica, accusing her of putting the welfare of the animals above his own needs.

Veronica bore it all in silence and did her best to placate him. However, things came to a head unexpectedly. One morning Veronica was out riding with Precious. They had not gone far when all of a sudden the horse stumbled and fell. Apparently a rodent had dug a hole and the horse stepped into it. Veronica was not hurt but oh, poor Precious!

Veronica ran back to the house screaming, "Ralph! Ralph! Help please!" He came out, took one look at the horse, went back for his gun, and with one shot and killed Precious. One moment she was there and the next she was gone.

Veronica was devastated, but she understood that when a horse is seriously hurt, the best thing is to kill it. What pushed her beyond her limit, though, was her husband's comment over his shoulder, as he walked away. "It's just as well. That will teach you not to get so attached to an animal. Come to the house. It's about time you did some cleaning!"

Veronica just stood there, tears streaming down her face and her chest convulsing with sobs. She had to get out of there! She turned around, walked back to the house, picked up her purse, got into her van, and drove off. For Veronica, standing up for herself and being assertive came before her fully formed vision.

In fact, she also used a support system to help her formulate her vision and commitment.

The Salvation Army happened to be in the nearest town, and the people there helped her find shelter. They also provided counseling and more support. Veronica, by rebooting her thinking, decided to take charge of her own life. In her vision, she would work with animals.

She learned that by being so submissive to Ralph, she had given him the power to abuse her. She made the commitment to her future self that such a thing would never happen again. With her assertiveness in place and accompanied by a law enforcement officer she drove back to the ranch. Ralph was working in the stables; he hadn't even bothered to go look for her. Veronica looked at him once, opened the screen door, went upstairs, and packed her belongings. Within minutes she came back out, got into her van, and never returned.

Veronica used her passion for animals to build her future. She moved to town, divorced her husband, and now has her own business boarding cats. She has rebooted her life! She is confident and smiling, and a picture of Precious hangs in her living room. "I am grateful and not taking anything for granted," she says, maintaining her vigilance against the old ways. Though in a different order, the five steps worked again.

Monique

Monique came to me when she heard I was looking for true-life stories about spouse abuse. Her first request was: "Don't use my name!" The second was: "Please listen. I need to vent but don't have the money to go to a counselor!"

Her dark expressive eyes were tearful when she said, "Look at me. Look at what I'm wearing." She was wearing faded jeans and a t-shirt. The sandals on her feet were old, I could see that. One strap was missing and the soles were brittle from use.

Monique told me that she had been married for ten years to a "really handsome guy." It was love at first sight for her. Raised in a strict religious environment, she hadn't dated much, and when Bob came along, she just knew he was the one for her. Bob, five years older than Monique, was the eldest of three brothers, and came from the same stern environment she had. They had met at a church function, where, as she said, "All the girls were in love with him because of his good looks, but he chose me!" While they were dating, she worked in a retail store and he worked in construction.

Soon after she graduated, they married, and he made her quit her job; Bob would provide for his family. Ironically, the couple had to live with his family until they saved enough for an apartment of their own, because in the five years since his graduation Bob didn't even have enough saved for a security deposit. They were very happy to get into their own place. It was where they would start the large family that Bob had already said he wanted.

One day as a playful newlywed, Monique grabbed the back of his belt and gave it a little tug. Immediately Bob turned around and gave her a vicious slap on her thigh, which turned bright red. "You need to know your place, woman, and the sooner you learn that the better." Looking back now, she told me she should have seen it coming. His mother was always silent and compliant.

Finally, after two years, Monique became pregnant but miscarried after the first trimester. The doctor told her she would never be able to have any children. Bob ranted and raved, telling her that it was her fault, making her feel not only heartsick, but alone. Instead of consoling her, Bob further isolated Monique by frequently having dinner at his parents' house, leaving Monique to eat by herself.

In addition, Bob insisted on selecting and buying Monique's clothes, when he decided what she had was worn out enough. So every once in a while he would bring her his taste in jeans, two or three t-shirts and some flip-flops. This was good enough for her because she wasn't working at a job anyway, so why should she care what she looked like? He monitored her visits to her parents and often accompanied her. Bob, of course, drove their only car.

"How did you get here," I asked her.

"By bus," she said, "and I can't stay long. I have to fix his supper."

"Have you talked to your parents about this? Surely you can talk on the phone when he isn't there?"

"Yes, I have," she said, "but my mother feels cherished by my dad. She doesn't get it. 'Give it time,' she told me, but how much time is necessary?"

She felt better after she and I talked, and was ready to go home. "It just isn't right," she said, "I want to leave."

"Please let me know once in a while how you are doing," I asked.

Several months later I received a phone call from Monique. By talking about the situation with me, she had developed a vision of life without abuse and made the commitment to make it happen. Using assertiveness she had been courageous enough to tell her husband how mistreated she felt and that she was leaving him. "He was speechless," she said with a laugh.

Living out her commitment she moved to another town and stayed with a relative who supplied the support she needed. There, through rebooting her thinking, she divorced her husband, got a job, went to counseling, and rebooted her life. Just like that! The new attitude she had developed inspired her to enroll at a community college, then get her four-year degree and become a kindergarten teacher. Today she has a strong circle of friends, her support system, and an active social life. She is vigilant about maintaining her new positive attitude, but not about her former husband. It turns out that her former husband no longer cares.

Patty

When I met Patty, a teacher, she was in a wheelchair. With difficulty, she rolled herself across her living room.

"I'm so glad you came," she said. Books and papers were strewn everywhere, and I saw that in the kitchen dirty dishes were stacked up in the sink and on the counter. "I just haven't got the strength to clean the house, but it wasn't this way before the accident." The accident had occurred ten years earlier during a ferocious thunderstorm. Patty had pulled off the road to the partial shelter of a tree. One bolt of lightning broke the tree in two. The upper half crushed her car and her spine, but she was alive. However, there would be no children.

She was a spunky lady and accepted that this was a change that she would have to adjust to and make the most of her life in spite of it.

"After all, you can still teach while in a wheelchair," she said.

The problem was her husband. When he heard about the accident, he rushed to her side and was supportive, telling her she would be fine and, with a little therapy, would be up and about in no time.

"But, Charles," she said. "tests have shown that I will never walk again. I know you wanted a large family and so did I, but maybe we can adopt children."

"Out of the question. Of course you will be able to have children."

Two years passed. Patty continued teaching and made peace with her new life. Charles did not. He began to scold her and humiliate her in public. When they got together with friends, they were always eager to help her get a drink or some food, but Charles would say, "This little woman can do much more that she lets you believe. Don't spoil her. She needs to learn. If she wanted to she could get out of the wheelchair and learn to walk again." Patty looked away because she couldn't bear to see the pity and outrage in the eyes of their friends.

After a while there were no more invitations, although Patty's friends phoned her quite often. Things got worse. "You can drive the van to work," he said, "why can't you clean the house?" Then Charles started to come home later and later. She became depressed but kept on teaching; that was what she loved to do. However, the stress sapped her strength and it was hard for her to remain cheerful and upbeat.

"I have to realize that Charles will leave me one day," she said, "and maybe that is for the best, but oh, I am so tired now, I can't take it anymore."

I encouraged her to start planning for her future by rebooting her thinking. The worst that could happen would be that Charles would divorce her. Would she be able to find an apartment that was wheelchair friendly? Would she be able to take care of herself and the place? "I know I could," she said. The mental vision brightened her eyes and lit up her face with a smile.

"Why don't you do some research now?" I suggested. "That way you will be prepared when the time comes."

I didn't hear from her until several years later. This time it was a different Patty! I could hear it immediately in her voice when she called.

"Til," she said, "I followed through with your advice and did some research, and it was a good thing that I did! Charles became more and more distant and through the grapevine I learned he was living with a girlfriend. In the beginning I was still devastated, but I realized that our marriage was no longer there. It was a blessing actually. When he was away, I didn't have to listen to his abuse."

"What did you do?" I asked.

Encouraged by her friends, her assertiveness showed when she stood up for herself and told him she wanted a divorce. Charles immediately agreed. "Thanks to all the research I did I now have my own apartment. It's small, so I can keep it neat. It's actually closer to my work. I get alimony and have my van. I'm quite content."

Patty continued, "I am now teaching at the university and have my sights set on becoming a tenured professor. She had a new vision! It will be a lot of work, but I have come this far and I am committed. I also have gathered a group of wheelchair bound students, and we meet once a week. We support and learn from each other, and I tell them not to be afraid to stand up for themselves. After all, that's what I did when I divorced my husband. I now feel in control of my life!

Patty was willing to do what it took; even a wheelchair couldn't hold her back! She has rebooted her life successfully.

Maria

Maria was born in Germany, but moved as a young woman to Toronto, where she went to work in a bank. One day she heard a familiar accent from a customer. Heinz too had come from Germany, where he was one of the great chefs. His wish was to go to New York and be employed there at one of the great hotels.

They started dating and moved to New York where he indeed became employed as a chef almost immediately. They married, money flowed, and life was good. Until she found out how terribly arrogant and controlling he was.

Maria worked until she became pregnant, and within two years they had two children. Heinz basked in the limelight at work and didn't want to be saddled with raising children. He developed a violent temper, lashed out at her and the children, and sometimes smashed the furniture. He often threatened to take the children back to Europe where he could find a job anywhere.

That did it! Maria wanted to escape this life! But she was smart, too. She told him she would call the hotel and tell them what kind of a chef they were employing. Of course his ego wouldn't permit that!

One day Heinz came home particularly violent. That was the last straw for Maria! She rebooted her thinking and created a vision for herself and her children to have a better life, and she made the commitment to her vision right then and there. She told him, "This is no longer acceptable. Please leave." Yes, she was standing up for herself! And Heinz left.

After 25 years of misery, she got a divorce and full custody of the two younger children with liberal visitation rights for her husband. Maria decided to go to Florida and start a new life. At first she worked as a masseuse, but that proved too hard on her. She had to find something else to do, so she formed a new vision. Because of her abusive life she had developed empathy for others, and she committed herself to finding a job that would feed her passion.

Maria put an ad in the local paper and quickly found a position taking care of elderly patients. With her alimony and her other income she is now able to support herself and feels very lucky. Secure in her own capabilities, she has set up a support system of wonderful friends, but she keeps up her vigilance. Her compassion for her fellow man should not be mistaken for vulnerability. She, too, has rebooted her life!

CONCLUSION

There are two important points that I want you to remember from this chapter.

First, when you meet a man who exhibits any of the above characteristics, do NOT get involved! Do NOT think that you can change him! These men are predators who take an intense pleasure in subjecting the woman to all kinds of abuse. They may be charming and considerate (like my first husband), but once married, their true character shows.

Second, take a look again at the various stories I related here. Betty, Monique, and Patty did some preliminary planning and research before they left their husbands. Veronica jumped right in! She just wanted to get away, and then through the help of her support system decided what to do with her life. Maria finally found her assertiveness when her husband threatened her safety and that of her children, and then she divorced him.

But they all had something in common. They all rebooted their thinking, meaning that they changed the way they looked at things. They all used the 5 steps although not necessarily in order (each had her own way of following through), and they all rebooted their lives successfully. You can, too.

Chapter Four

PARENTAL ABUSE

How often have you heard the old saying "Sticks and stones may break my bones but words will never hurt me"? Is it really true? Obviously not. All we have to do is look at the news to see the reports on both children and adults killing themselves because of this kind of bullying.

And I know it isn't true from my own experience. Emotional and verbal abuse leaves deep marks. They are sometimes referred to as invisible scars, but in truth they are often really invisible wounds; they are still raw and haven't healed, perhaps because the assaults haven't stopped, or the words are still playing on the mind. The result is that the child sees himself or herself as powerless and has a very low self-esteem. If nothing is done to break this cycle, the child grows up to be an adult who most probably will experience any or all of the following:

l. Lack of trust and relationship difficulties

If you can't trust your parents, whom can you trust? Without a secure childhood it is very difficult to learn to trust people or know who is trustworthy.

This can lead not only to future abusive relationships (this is all the child has ever known), but also to difficulty maintaining relationships due to fear of being controlled or abused.

2. Feelings of being "worthless" or "damaged"

If people have been told over and over as children (like I was) that they are stupid or no good, it is very difficult to overcome these feelings. The child will see them as reality. As adults the victims may feel so worthless that they don't want to get the education that will help them realize their true potential, so they settle for low-paying jobs, reaffirming their low opinion of themselves. Deep down they feel they "can't do it anyway." Sexual abuse survivors often struggle with the feeling of being damaged, and not worthy of good jobs or respect.

3. Trouble with handling emotions

Abused children have trouble expressing emotions. As a result, emotions get suppressed, appearing later in unexpected ways that may be self-sabotaging and threatening to others. These children can struggle with anxiety, depression, or anger. They may turn to alcohol or drugs to numb the painful feelings. In my case, my emotions damaged my body, resulting in Post Traumatic Stress Disorder.

MYTHS ABOUT EMOTIONAL AND VERBAL ABUSE

Because the damage done by parental emotional and verbal – that is, *mental* – abuse can't be seen, people sometimes think it doesn't exist. Nothing could be further from the truth. Let me also put to rest some of these myths.

- **Myth l: It's abuse only if it is violent.**

  Fact: Physical abuse is just one type of abuse.

- **Myth 2: Only bad people abuse their children that way.**

  Fact: It's not always so clear-cut. Not all abusers are intentionally harming their children. Many have been victims of abuse themselves and don't know any other way to parent. (My parents were abused as children and consequently didn't know any better, but I didn't discover that until I was much, much older!) But that doesn't mean that it's okay for them to go on doing it.

- **Myth 3: Mental abuse doesn't happen in "good" families.**

  Fact: Mental abuse crosses all racial, economic, and cultural lines. Sometimes, families who seem to have it all are hiding a different reality. My parents were a prime example – perfect to the outside world, but inside the house they were very destructive to their child.

Here are some stories of people who were verbally and emotionally abused by one or both parents and how they escaped the chain of abuse.

Thea

I met Thea when I was visiting relatives in the Netherlands. She had grown up in the eastern part of Holland, close to the German border. We discovered that we were the same age and had similar war experiences, so we frequently met for coffee.

Thea was the middle child of nine siblings and had lived her childhood on a farm. Her soft-spoken father was a cabinetmaker who didn't want to make waves. He had his own workshop where he spent most of his time. Her mother, a homemaker, was quite different. Loud, angry, and unapproachable, she had borne nine children in quick succession and, as Thea put it, "Lost it then." She pushed the children away when they came to her and did little positive parenting, often ridiculing them.

Thea remembers her mother told her on several occasions that she was "too ugly" to find herself a man and she would do well to find a job and stick to it. Since the children were left to their own devices, they fought among themselves and, in order to escape harsh punishment, tattled about each other to their mother. Thea often woke up to the screams, slaps, and fighting among her brothers and sisters.

The only way she could escape the mayhem at her home was to walk into the forest and just sit there. She had her own private place where she went and railed many times against a God who made her life so miserable.

After high school Thea worked in a bank and never looked at any man because it was so ingrained in her that she was "ugly." Eventually she did marry. But as so often happens, she was so glad someone found her pretty enough to propose to that she did not question his intentions, and said "yes" almost right away. (Spouse abusers often push their victims into a commitment very quickly.) Little did she realize that he too was abusive and controlling. He divorced her eight years later and she has not remarried since. She feels fortunate that they didn't have children.

All her life many people had worked to break Thea's spirit, but by rebooting her thinking she was able to reboot her life. First, she found her vision. She loved the water and saw herself living on a small houseboat filled with potted plants and moored in a quiet canal. Then she made the commitment to stand up for herself as much as was necessary to make her dream a reality. With her divorce settlement she was able to do just that. The gentle lapping of the waves against her little boat gave her a measure of peace.

After a while she realized that she needed more. She found a nearby church that she liked where people were friendly and interested in her. They became her positive network – her support system – something she had never experienced before! It wasn't long before she realized she really had a lot to offer the world.

Thea was grateful that she was able to escape from a life of abuse and realized she had the empathy to help others. This opened up new possibilities for her, and she formed a new vision. She changed her views about God and decided to become a minister. She enrolled in seminary and committed herself to her studies. Four years later she graduated with a B.A. in Theology, and today she has her own little church with members who add to her support system.

Thea is thrilled with her new life, but she's smart enough to know that old ways of thinking can creep back insidiously. Thea maintains her vigilance so she can maintain the success that others had tried to keep from her.

Carol

Carol had quite a different story. Her mother had always wanted two children, a girl for herself and a boy for her husband Roger. She hoped that a son would give him a sense of purpose. The first child was a girl, Alice, and her mother was elated! Two years later Carol was born. Her mother was so upset that she had had another girl that she kept saying, "Oh, my poor Roger!" He worked hard six days a week and was not much involved in the rearing of his two little girls, but he loved Carol for herself. Ironically, he really didn't care which gender she was!

Carol grew up in the shadow of her older sister, who was their mother's pet. When Alice needed a haircut, she was taken to the best beautician. When Carol needed a haircut, she was taken to the local barber! She never got new clothes but had to wear hand-me-downs from Alice. Alice's coloring was totally different from Carol's, and so Carol had to wear the most unbecoming colors.

Out of desperation Carol began to eat. Food was her escape both from her mother and from her sister's clothes. Unfortunately being heavy was a burden (in more ways than one) that she had to carry for most of her life. Alice had become a spoiled child and, unlike Carol, was popular in school. When the sisters had disagreements, it was no use talking to their mother. She would invariably take Alice's side.

After high school, Carol wanted to write and find a career in publishing, but her mother pooh-poohed the idea, and that was that. She was allowed to go to college and became a high school teacher because her parents wanted her to "always be able to support herself." When she graduated the only thing her mother said was, "Well, at least you now have a title behind your name."

Carol taught for many years. Her parents divorced, and her mother mercifully went to live with her favored daughter and her husband. When Carol's father took ill, she saw a means of escape, quit her job, and took care of him for several years. And he appreciated her. When he died, Carol's mother and sister didn't think it necessary to come down for the funeral because they were going on a cruise.

 Carol now lives quite happily by herself in the house her father left her. She rebooted her life by rebooting her thinking. A doctor she went to see taught her to envision herself becoming slim. She committed to going to Overeaters Anonymous and lost more than 50 pounds. She also stood up for herself enough to cut off all relations with her mother and sister.

The emotional sustenance she should have gotten from them has been replaced by a broad support system. She organized a book club, plays cards, still attends Overeaters Anonymous – and adopted a cat. Support systems come in many forms.

Carol's eyes sparkled when she showed me her new clothes – in smaller sizes and in colors that are right for her. "Of course, Til," she said, "I will always have to watch out. Put 10 cookies in front of me and I will probably eat them!" Vigilance, too, comes in many forms.

Dawn

Dawn and her twin sister Donna were adopted when they were two years old. Soon after their adoption, their new parents changed their first names. They were now Patricia and Joan! The girls were very confused and often cried together in their bedroom.

Their new mother, a former teacher, homeschooled the girls and had very little patience with them. She wanted bright, beautiful girls and simply could not understand why they didn't understand their lessons right away! Dawn remembers when she was six years old, she didn't quite master her addition and subtraction, and her mother was furious. She was made to stand in a corner and called "dummy" several times while Donna struggled on the best she could.

Their father would leave home whenever there was a scene and did nothing to help them. When they were a little older, he took them outside one day and said: "If it wasn't for you girls, I would have killed myself a long time ago." This, of course, put an extra burden on them.

Dawn and Donna had few friends. Their mother kept them close to home, always giving them extra homework or chores to do. "We could never please her, no matter how hard we tried," said Dawn.

Eventually, the girls were old enough to escape from this intolerable situation. Dawn got her license as a nursing assistant but suffered from chronic depression. Donna found a job as a secretary. The two girls stayed away from their mother and had little to do with their father, who died fairly soon after they left home.

Their mother became a bitter old woman, blaming everything on everyone but herself. She delighted in trying to stir up trouble between the girls, but they were too close. Dawn eventually married Fred, but he turned out to be as controlling and abusive as her mother. "I had jumped from the frying pan into the fire," Dawn said. Then Donna, her only confidant, died unexpectedly, and Dawn's health began to deteriorate. She had to quit her job as a nursing assistant and started going to counseling. She missed her sister terribly.

During one of her counseling sessions Dawn remembered that *Patricia* was not her birth name. She did some research, tracked down an old birth certificate, and discovered that her real name was *Dawn* and her sister's name was *Donna!*

"Til," she said, "It was as if I could see a new woman. For me the word 'Dawn' had a special meaning, a new beginning, a new day. It was a wonderful feeling! I had this vision of a woman, one who was free of the abuse she had endured from her adoptive mother, one who wasn't afraid to speak up, who didn't behave like a mouse."

At night she was rebooting her thinking by repeating over and over, "I am Dawn, not Patricia, I am a new woman." And she rebooted her life when she began to stand up for herself. It took courage to speak up but here she was, in Fred's office and actually facing him! She told him her name was no longer Patricia but Dawn and he should call her that. To her surprise he didn't seem to mind. But his response confirmed his mean spirit. "I don't care what your name is, as long as you toe the line," he snapped.

She made a list of things she thought were important for her to grow spiritually, and she converted to Catholicism. When she got involved with one of her church's women's groups, they became a support system for her. They soon put her on one of their committees. She was expected to carry her own weight, which meant she couldn't back out without "feeling like a mouse again." She made another commitment, to follow through with those obligations, and she is proud that she is sticking to it.

Dawn has made several friends in her group who cheer her on when she isn't sure she can keep going. She keeps thinking of the abuse she and Donna suffered at the hands of their adoptive mother. "You don't undo all those years of abuse overnight," she says. But her support group is in place and she has phone numbers of friends she can call at any time.

It is still hard for Dawn to make decisions on her own. Fred's abusive behavior makes it difficult for her to speak her mind, so learning to stand up for herself is one of the things she is still working on because she has decided she will not divorce him.

Because she is inclined to be a pleaser, Dawn sometimes accepts tasks but then lets them slide because of her health. However, last week when she was asked to make phone calls for her women's group, "I had to take a deep breath, but I told them I would not be able to do it. I have to be vigilant about my health all the time," she says, "But Dawn is definitely here to stay!"

Jody

Jody was the only child in an upscale family. Her father was a lawyer and her mother a well-known fund-raiser. They were seldom home and young Jody was raised by her nanny Carla. In Jody's early years Carla was for all intents and purposes her mother. Carla loved her and took total care of her, which was fine with Jody's parents.

They made sure to enroll their daughter in the best pre-schools, which of course would later lead to the best schools and colleges. Jody also had a cat, Timmy, and between Carla and Timmy her early years were fine. Sadly, when Jody turned six, Carla was let go and Jody was devastated. So her parents bought her expensive presents; in fact she could have anything she wanted as long as she kept out of their hair. "You see, Til," she said, "I was not so much verbally abused as emotionally abused."

Her parents had their own lives and Jody sometimes wondered why they even had a child. One day when she was about nine years old, she mustered all her courage and asked her father, "Why? Why did you have me if you're never around?" Her father replied, "Because it was expected of us." What a downer! She felt she was born only for show!

Early on there was a string of babysitters. Later, when Jody became a teenager, she came home to an empty house and warmed something up for dinner. She was not allowed to have friends over and became quiet. She could not relate to the typical behaviors of her classmates who thought her strange and aloof. So she came to be an outsider.

Jody had suppressed her feelings for so long she didn't even realize that deep down there was still that little girl who wanted to cry and laugh and be wanted by her parents.

She went to college (one of the best of course) and met Pat, a counselor who understood what had happened in her life. She took a special interest in Jody and became a warm, caring friend. "If it hadn't been for Pat," she said, "I would probably have ended my life. I was that lonely and depressed."

Little by little Jody rebooted her thinking and her life. She learned to smile, and pretty soon she attracted a circle of friends. Pat made her see that she could make a future for herself. Jody's vision was to become a lawyer and then a family court judge. She committed to the long-term goal to do what it took. With strength and by standing up for herself, she is making good on that promise.

She learned to have fun as well, and has lots of friends as her support system. Jody is now a defense lawyer in family court. And as for being vigilant? "I don't have to worry about that," she laughs, "This is my life's work and there is no way I will return to being unhappy. By the way," she adds, "I don't see my parents anymore. I have escaped from that environment. They are relieved and so am I."

Claire

I met Claire and her sister Kate at a party. It was one of those New Year's parties where alcohol is served and there is lots to eat. Claire, her sister, and her brother had grown up in New York, but she and Kate had recently moved to a southern state and bought a house together. When I remarked upon the fact that neither one of them was drinking alcohol, Claire told me the following story.

Their parents, now deceased, had been good people. Although not wealthy, they provided their kids with a happy childhood, except when they drank. In the beginning it was not much of a problem, and the care of the children was steady and consistent.

Over the years, however, the parents' behavior changed. It was their drinking that became steady and consistent, and a huge problem. Slowly but surely they stopped caring for their children. Claire's father hid his alcoholism well at work, but her mom could no longer hide the bottles and, when drunk, would lash out at her children.

Claire said that in the beginning the three of them could cope, but eventually their grades dropped, they looked unkempt, and they began to stick together against the world around them. What saved them in the end was an intervention by Child Protective Services which put them in foster care. They attended Alateen and learned about the disease that had taken hold of their parents. They lived in foster care for several years, separated, but still in touch with each other.

Claire's father died at a fairly young age of cirrhosis of the liver, and her mother had to be put in a nursing home because she had developed Alzheimer's disease. When Claire was eighteen, she rebooted her thinking and went to college, determined to make something of herself. She visualized herself as a social worker, and her commitment not to fall into the alcohol trap has served her well.

Her brother, unfortunately, has not been able to hold a job and drifts around the country; he too has begun to drink. Kate has rebooted her thinking and is doing well. She has just begun to attend college and looks up to her older sister. Both girls have rebooted their lives!

Claire, having learned to stand up for herself and to say *no* when offered a drink, tells it like it is. "Either you have a vision of where you see yourself, or you will drift just like my brother." Both sisters know about this disease and have friends (their support system) who aren't caught up by the dangers of alcohol. They are glad they have escaped the threat of alcoholism so far, but they are always vigilant not to fall into the same trap. As Claire says, "We only have to look at our brother to keep ourselves on the straight and narrow."

Claire frequently gives lectures about alcoholism and the abuse she and her siblings experienced when they were young. She ends with this point: Her parents were basically good people who really cared about their children until they began to care about alcohol more.

Regrettably parents often don't realize that the alcohol they drink can change them into something they don't want to be. In addition, they may never give a thought to the fact that the alcohol they drink can also change their children into something they don't want *them* to be.

CONCLUSION

There are many types of abuse that parents can perpetrate on their children. Parents may neglect their children or treat them in ways that tell the children that they have no value. Parents may be highly demanding or set bad examples of how to live.

Unfortunately parents may indulge in more than one of these behaviors. Of course this devastates the children and their childhood years, but the effects don't end when the children get older.

Often the severe emotional damage to abused children does not fully surface until adolescence or even later. Adults who were abused as children often have trouble establishing lasting and stable personal relationships. They are also at higher risk for anxiety, depression, substance abuse, medical illness, and problems at school or work.

However, by rebooting your thinking, following the five steps – and thereby rebooting your life – you will be able to overcome the damage inflicted in previous years.

Chapter Five

BULLYING BY CHILDREN

Bullying has probably been around for as long as people have, but only recently has it risen to the level of mainstream media coverage. It can happen in backyards and front yards, but a huge number of incidents happen or start in schools and school yards.

Consider the following United States statistics:

- Surveys show that 77% of students are bullied mentally, verbally, or physically.
- 1 out of five kids admits to being a bully.
- 100,000 students carry a gun to school on a regular basis.
- 28% of youths who carried weapons have witnessed violence at home.
- Playground statistics when a child is bullied: adult intervention 4%, peer intervention 11%, *no intervention 85%.*

Here's another horrifying statistic from the United Kingdom, which is a very small country compared to the United States: each year, at least 16 children kill themselves because they are being bullied at school *and no one in authority* is doing anything serious about it. Failure by a school to implement an effective, active anti-bullying policy is absolutely a breach of duty of care.

THE REASONS FOR BULLYING

When bullying is reported, a strictly superficial reason is often cited as the cause of bullying. Just about anything can be the apparent – but not actual – cause a child is picked on; for example, being fat, thin, tall, short; skin color; wearing glasses; having big ears, crooked teeth, the "wrong" clothes (I wore homemade clothes); and an unwillingness to use strength to defend oneself.

However, bullying is not caused by the victim. Rather it comes from some circumstance relating to the bully himself or herself. It can be the need for attention, defensiveness to avoid becoming a bullying victim himself or herself, or living in an abusive environment. For children growing up in a dysfunctional or abusive home environment, bullying can become a compulsive and obsessive behavior.

The bully simply has to have a target onto whom he or she can displace his or her own aggression. The bully's parents may not care enough about what is going on to try to correct it. Or, the parents may lack parenting skills because they too were brought up by parents who lacked appropriate skills and their parents were brought up the same way (and so it passes from one generation to the next).

Crista Wetherington, Ph.D. and a pediatric psychologist, states that bullying can have such a significant and long-term impact on children and teenagers who are being bullied that it can even contribute to eating disorders, self-injury, and other self-sabotaging behaviors.

The cycle needs to be broken.

Here are characteristics typical of a bully:

- Aggression
- Physical strength
- Poor social skills
- Low self-esteem
- Insecurities
- Need to impress
- Disrespect and contempt for others (not only children but adults as well)

Once bullying starts, many other children side with the bully because they know that otherwise they too will be bullied. The bully rules through fear and his "entourage" knows it!

Sadly, childhood roles play on into adulthood. There is a lot of evidence to suggest that the child who learns to bully at school and gets away with it goes on to be the serial bully in the workplace. Likewise, the child who is bullied at school also goes on to be a likely target of bullying in the workplace.

Petra

Petra, who grew up in Holland, told me the following story. During WWII, when she was a young girl, she was bullied unmercifully. "You see," she said, "my parents were thought to be collaborators with the Germans. Adults and children shunned us all, but I, having to go to school each day, got the worst of it."

Here is Petra's story in her own words.

"We lived in a small village where everyone knew each other and it was no secret that I was the daughter of, you know, those people, those dirty collaborators. What people didn't know was that my parents were forced to attend Nazi meetings because my father's boss was a true collaborator. My father would have lost his job and starved like the other village people if he refused to go. Yes, I know, he could have opted for that, but he didn't, and so he became a supporter of the Nazis, at least by reputation. This was enough, of course. Word got around and so I ended up with years of hell.

"There were three big girls who were always lying in wait for me. I couldn't escape. They would follow me to school, singing a dirty song about what would happen to people who 'loved' the Germans, pelting me with garbage, stones, anything they could get their hands on, and so I would arrive in school looking dirty, crying, and often without my books, which they had ripped out of my arms. Teachers were well aware of what was going on but did nothing. My parents were afraid to intervene because they had their own troubles. I didn't have any friends either."

One day Petra had had enough. She allowed herself to think about what she would like her life to be and how she could make it happen.

"I had a vision of what it would feel like to have friends, to walk to school with them and to arrive with clean clothes. I committed to the idea and devised a plan to make it become a reality. Instead of wearing one set of clothing, I would wear two, one on top of the other! I had thought about putting clean clothes in my backpack, but quite often my pack would be torn and they would see I had a change of clothes in there.

"So I picked a day to try my plan. When I arrived dirty, I took off my dirty clothes in the restroom and shoved them in my pack, washed my face, combed my hair, and got into my seat. You should have seen the faces of the others! It made me feel so good, I even sat up straight in my chair!"

Yes! That was Petra being assertive and standing up for herself!

"I stuck to my plan and slowly one or two of my classmates began to smile at me. Instead of a beaten down, sobbing, dirty girl, they now saw a nice clean girl who smiled back at them. The majority of the class still sided with the bullies, but even during recess I now could talk and play with a few of them."

Petra was forming her support system.

"You know what I noticed? The more friends I acquired, the less I was bullied because now it was not three against one but three against three or even more! I began to stand up straight and walk with some confidence, knowing I was no longer alone but had some friends to support me. I could tell them that I hated Germans just as much as they did and that I couldn't help what my parents were.

"Towards the end of the war, things were much better and I even enjoyed going to class. Those bullies still taunted me and I will remember that to the end of my days, but it seemed that the sport of beating up on a little girl had lost some of its allure. I was never popular, but that was okay. In your terms, Til, I had rebooted my thinking and therefore had rebooted my life. I became willing to do what it took to develop my backbone enough to make it through school. And now I pay attention every day to maintaining that backbone." That's what being vigilant is all about.

Joanne

Joanne was teased and bullied all during her school years, but the worst were her elementary school days. She was an only child and had a very aggressive mother who harassed the teachers and principal with numerous complaints. Joanne often died of embarrassment, and wished she could escape! The other kids picked up on this immediately, of course, and one of them, a girl named Tina, was especially mean. She had black hair which she wore long and loose. All the girls envied her and did their best to become part of her group.

Tina and Joanne lived not too far from each other so after school they walked the same street to go home. It was Tina's nasty habit to walk behind Joanne, run up to her, and pull her hair or punch her in the back, always with a sneer on her face. When Joanne turned around, she would dance away, giggle, and pretend nothing had happened.

One day it was just too much. Joanne whirled around, dropped her books, twisted a handful of that long black hair around her fist, and tugged as hard as she could. Tina screamed and, because they were now close together, she kicked upwards and broke Joanne's pinkie. Joanne didn't even notice it till later because now she had a lovely hunk of hair in her hand! It was a great feeling! Joanne's vision began to form.

Not long after that Joanne was invited to a birthday party. This was new to her; she had always been left out, but she went out of curiosity. When she arrived, imagine her surprise to find most of the popular girls there, including Tina. "What am I doing here?" she wondered.

After refreshments, they all trooped up to Tina's bedroom, and there it was immediately clear. Joanne was supposed to duke it out with Tina, with the rest of the girls cheering for Tina, of course.

Joanne recalled her vision from her success of grabbing long hair and that deep feeling of satisfaction. The pinkie was forgotten, and the fight began. Tina fought hard and everyone expected her to win. But somehow Joanne got her arm around Tina's neck and was able to twist her to the ground and sit on her. What a victory!

Everyone was stunned. That was not supposed to happen. And Tina never accosted her again.

Joanne's school years improved dramatically because she now knew she could deal with the bullying. Interestingly, she never fought again – maybe because no one else wanted to take the chance of being humiliated by her.

After graduation she took a secretarial job with the vision of getting into management. She was standing up for herself when she asked for a raise and got it. That made another decision possible. She committed herself to going to college at night, and she eventually got a degree in marketing.

Today Joanne is assistant manager of a department store. No doubt her outgoing and friendly personality will help her make it to the top. She is gracious and friendly. She has made it a priority to have a strong support system with lots of friends and to network regularly. She knows that by rebooting her thinking, she has rebooted her life. She is proud of herself.

"I was willing to do what needed to be done," she said, "and it all started with pulling out a hunk of long, black hair!"

Belinda

When I met Belinda, I was immediately impressed! She was a tall, friendly girl with smiling eyes. Belinda owned her own business, was married, and had two sons. Her family was obviously very important to her. "It was not always that way," Belinda confided. Then she extended her right arm and I noticed she had a prosthesis.

Belinda had been born with a normal left arm but with only a stub of a right arm. Raised in foster care she had lived with many families. She admitted she had been a handful when she was younger because her handicap had made her angry and difficult to get along with. Although she knew she needed help, she was too proud to ask for it, and quite often created difficulties for her foster parents by sneaking out of the house at night. "I tried to get away from everybody," she said.

In school, it was much of the same. Teachers looked away when she was bullied, especially during PE when she was only partially able to participate. Other children taunted her with the nickname Stump. One day, during class, the boy who sat behind her, pinched her stump. Belinda flew into a rage, grabbed a ruler, and smashed it down onto the boy's hand, breaking a bone. She had gone beyond assertive to aggressive.

That was the end for her, in one way, but it also turned out to be a beginning. Social Services was called and she was placed in a girls' home where there was strict discipline. It was there, she said, that she found a counselor who was willing to listen and to work with her. For the first time in her life, Belinda had found a friend. Instead of continuing to be the angry girl she had always been, she was shown ways to channel that anger.

This knowledge gave her the courage to create the vision of graduating from high school, which she did with honors. She made it a commitment and planned how to stand up for herself and attract a support system of friends. She had rebooted her thinking and thereby rebooted her life; it worked!

Then, to her utter surprise, came the best present she had ever had. She was taken to a specialist who fitted her with a prosthesis. It took a while to get used to, but it changed her life forever. She knew that she never wanted to return to her old attitudes and behaviors again, and she maintains her vigilance to ensure it.

The new enthusiasm created by the success prompted her to create a new vision: going to college and using the same successful process to become a fashion designer. In her free time she worked as an apprentice learning how to design clothes, and also made herself available as a "big sister." It was her way to pay forward what her counselor had done for her. Belinda never wavered in her plans and today owns her own business. She is respected in her community and, as she says, "I feel like a new woman, both inside and out."

Beatrice

When Beatrice was born, she was not what you would call a pretty baby. Her eyes were crossed, she couldn't see very well, and she had a cleft palate. Her feet also turned inwards. Bea and her older brother Peter were only 22 months apart.

When their mother took them on their daily outing, they were put together in a large stroller and people often stopped to admire the babies until they got a closer look at Bea. With pity in their eyes they would make some remarks about how healthy she looked and how beautiful Peter was.

The family didn't have much money and couldn't afford health insurance, but they managed to scrape enough together to have Bea's mouth repaired. "It left us almost broke," their mother said. It was an immediate improvement for Bea, but still there was the matter of her eyes and feet.

Peter and Bea were homeschooled until Peter was five and then he went to public school. Bea was inconsolable, but her mother held her close and told her she would go soon as well. It was her plan meanwhile to consult with a specialist who could perhaps straighten out her daughter's feet. She and her husband knew surgery was not an option and so it was decided that Bea would wear special heavy boots that would gradually turn her feet right side out. She hated those shoes!

Finally it was Bea's turn to go to school and she was so excited! The teacher had been forewarned that Bea couldn't see very well and that she looked different with her heavy boots. But when she got home, she was sobbing. "Everyone looked at me," she hiccuped and there was even a boy who made fun of my eyes! Mom, am I ugly?"

"There was nothing I could do or say," said her mother, "so I just held her."

Over the years Bea's appearance improved. Her feet straightened out and the scar on her mouth faded, but her eyes were still crossed and she was wearing glasses with thick lenses. The bullying continued all through high school. She became withdrawn and sensitive about her appearance.

However, learning came easy to Bea and she brought home As on a regular basis. This made the bullying even worse. "Hey, little dolly, did you get another A? It's too bad that you're so ugly. I bet no one has ever dated you!" On and on it went and teachers turned a blind eye. "Oh, I wanted to get away from that school in the worst possible way," she said.

Because Bea was smart, the school counselor urged her to go to college and get a degree in Special Education. "You will always have a job. They need teachers who have gone through what you've gone through," the counselor said. Bea did some serious thinking (she rebooted her mind), went to college, and graduated with a degree in psychology. That's what she wanted, to become a child psychologist.

Her practice flourished because she had a special empathy for children with problems. Her self-esteem grew as a direct result. Parents were grateful for her help and Bea began to see herself as a worthwhile human being. She had rebooted her life! She also began to see herself as beautiful, not only on the inside but on the outside as well.

Bea developed a vision of herself with perfect 20/20 eyes and committed to a plan to have a procedure to straighten her eyes and another procedure to correct her vision. This decision made her realize how much she had grown and made her proud of the fact she could stand up for herself.

Her family supported her wholeheartedly and both surgeries were successful. Bea couldn't believe how different she looked and declared she would no longer be plain old Bea; now she was Beatrice. The ugly duckling had turned into a swan!

Seeing her clients everyday is a constant reminder to Beatrice of how she felt when she was their age. She maintains her vigilance because she must walk her talk not only for herself, but for her patients.

Kaylee

Kaylee and her two brothers were raised by a single parent. Her father left his family soon after she was born, and had very little contact with his children. They lived in a small town with one public school with few extra services. Money was scarce and her mother had to work two jobs to keep their head above water, leaving her two older sons to look after their little sister. This usually was no problem. Brad and Keith loved their little sister and their mother knew that Kaylee was in good hands. Both boys attended public school and did well.

Kaylee was a little different. She was not exactly retarded, but it took her much longer to absorb lessons and directions. She was short for her age and obese. "A little butterball," her mother said affectionately. Kaylee had a beautiful smile, though, and when she looked at others, they couldn't help but love her. Regular classes were very hard for her but she struggled on. She was kept back several times and when word got out that she was eleven and still in third grade for the second time the abuse became never ending.

"Hey you, retard, why don't you go back to kindergarten?" Or: "Can you count to ten? Show us." And when Kaylee, innocently, began to count "One, two, three…" her tormentors burst out laughing. Kaylee didn't understand at first but when they began to push and shove her, she got scared, burst into tears, and ran out of the school. She wanted to escape the bullies, and she didn't want to go back. Her mother went to the principal and requested a meeting with Kaylee's teachers. It was clear that she couldn't go on that way, and it was decided that arrangements would be made to have her attend a special education school in a nearby town. Fortunately transportation was available.

From that day on Kaylee's life turned around. She was happy in her new school and made good progress. She graduated when she was twenty years old.

I recently saw her mom and asked what she was doing now. "She is working in an office, would you believe it? She has learned to file and is doing well. It is a repetitive job, of course, but that is just right for her. She is cheerful and happy and has recently started looking for a boyfriend!"

People like Kaylee don't consciously have a vision or reboot their thinking but the principle remains the same. When she saw the opportunity to succeed, she did so wholeheartedly and that was her commitment and her self-confidence. Her special school became her support system and, because she wanted to do well, she has rebooted her life!

CONCLUSION

The lives of Petra, Joanne, Belinda, Beatrice and Kaylee demonstrate that people who were bullied as children can overcome the likely consequences, if they can develop an effective process, use it, and maintain outside support.

In a report on bullying, Dr. Ronald Pitner, Ph.D., professor of social work at the Washington University in St. Louis, Missouri, concluded that schools must focus on the physical setting of the school. Dr. Pitner noted that bullying and school violence typically occur in predictable locations within schools, such as hallways, restrooms, stairwells and playgrounds. He believes that schools can cut down on violence if they identify the specific "hot spots."

Although this approach will not completely eliminate bullying, it certainly cuts down the areas of opportunity where bullying is likely to occur. The result is not only a safer learning climate, but an environment where bullies learn to live without bullying, their would-be hangers-on never experience that role, and their targets are spared humiliation and baggage they carry to adulthood.

Chapter Six

WORKPLACE ABUSE

Workplace abuse is the kind of abuse people don't often talk about. It happens behind "closed doors," office doors that is. It can be perpetrated by a boss or by a colleague. It can be an annoying or life altering. No matter who does it or how serious the effects are, workplace abuse is wrong and should be stopped.

When it happened to me for the first time, I was young, naïve, and utterly taken by surprise. I thought at first that my supervisor was joking, and so the best I could do was to pretend something hadn't been said. However, when it continued, I could no longer pretend, but calling him on it was out of the question because I didn't want to lose my job. I began to dread going to work and stopped talking with my co-workers. They all knew, of course, and I knew they knew.

Workplace abuse is still prevalent, but I hope that the stories of the five women in this chapter will become an inspiration to any woman who suffers from this kind of abuse.

Pamela Lutgen-Sandvik, Ph.D. and professor at the University of Arizona, gives the following definition of workplace abuse:

"Workplace abuse is distinguished from regular impoliteness by a longer duration, greater frequency, greater intensity and (usually) some type of power disparity.

"It is much more severe than typical gripes at work, especially when exerted on those in lesser positions of power within a company. This can, for example, be a supervisor of a group of employees abusing his or her power to isolate and demoralize subordinates. The abusive employee constantly offends the victim, creating a hostile work environment."

Employees who are abused at work have a difficult time, even when the abuse comes from someone who isn't in a higher position. They often dread going to work every day and are left in a state of confusion as to why they cannot defend themselves, according to Lutgen-Sandvik and colleagues in the September 2007 *Journal of Management Studies.* She states that employees who endure workplace abuse have, predictably, experienced more stress, anxiety, depression, and other mental health problems than those who don't have to face it.

Workplace abuse affects both men and women. It comprises five different categories, as Jaimee Marsh and colleagues explain in a study published in *Journal of Occupational Health* in 2009.

- Threats and bribes
- Isolation and exclusion
- Verbal aggression
- Disrespectful behaviors
- Physical aggression

When interviewed, about one quarter of employees disclosed being abused at work. They also note that women are more susceptible to abuse than men and the effects are worse on women. Specifically they are more likely to experience negative impacts on health and social relationships. Women of color are even more at risk for such negative consequences, especially when they have positions of higher rank or are in positions that do not fit stereotypical roles, the research shows.

Nell

Nell, a young woman who experienced verbal aggression and disrespectful behavior in her department, managed to improve work conditions not just for herself, but for everyone.

Several years ago Nell, who had an MBA, joined a small but growing company as a junior executive. Her supervisor liked her. Both she and the board of directors were impressed with Nell's work and constantly told her she would go far in their company. She blossomed under all that praise and gave 100%, as she was brought up to do.

The trouble was with her co-workers. Some of them had been there far longer than Nell and were used to doing things their way. "Don't rock the boat," they told her many times. However, Nell was a bright young woman with an inquisitive mind. She experimented with different ways to streamline procedures, and in her enthusiasm stepped on many toes. People began to talk about her, gossiped behind her back, and called her the teacher's pet and even a hooker. However, she never spoke up to any of them.

One day she was called in by her supervisor and asked to explain what was going on. The morale in the department was low and work did not get finished on time. In a meeting, her co-workers aired all their gripes and concerns, and then she was given the opportunity to state her case.

Nell was a quick study; she formed her Vision on the spot. "By listening to you all I now realize that I have not been a team player," she said. "I am new here and should not have tried to do things only my way. I apologize to every one of you. How about," she said with a smile, "if we all envision a smoothly run, effective department? We could blend my ways with yours and make a commitment to work together. If you have a concern, you can speak up and we all will listen and come to a consensus. We can support each other and make this the best run department in the company. Of course we all will have to work to keep it that way!"

Nell told me that people looked at her doubtfully at first, but the idea seemed to appeal to some, and by the end of the meeting they decided to give it a try.

"Would you believe our department won an award the next year because productivity was up, morale was high, and absenteeism was low!" she exulted. "We have a great bunch of people here!"

Nell not only used the 5-step process to stop abuse from being heaped on her, but she extended it to bring out the best in others. She adapted the process in such a way that the lives of a whole office full of people was improved. They all had rebooted their thinking and thereby rebooted their lives. A side benefit was that all of these folks also learned by example the lesson of how beneficial (that is, cool) it is to bring everyone onboard for a project and keep them there.

Margot

Margot was a shy, introverted woman. Her father had died when she was very young and she and her two older sisters were raised by a mother who was very reserved by nature. The age difference between her sisters and her was such that she felt more or less like an only child. Margot was mechanically inclined and went to college to become an engineer, but she had no friends to speak of. She kept to herself and was lonely; somehow she could not get outside her "comfort zone" and talk to people.

The apartments on either side of hers were occupied by women who knew each other and often hung over their balconies shouting to each other. This made her feel all the more left out, but she just couldn't get the courage up to talk with them.

Margot also felt that she was not "a quick thinker" as she put it. She was deliberate and took her time thinking about the engineering problems she was working on. Conscientious in her work, she often worked late hours. Since she had no hobbies to speak of, she sometimes even went to work on weekends simply because it gave her something to do.

Her co-workers mostly ignored her, but there was one person who took great delight in abusing her. "Hey, Margot, did you move? I thought you were dead!" Or: "Do you see that, everyone? Margot has just picked up her pencil. Let's celebrate!" On and on it went, and nobody did anything to stop it. She internalized every hurt and spiteful word and was even toying with the idea of suicide when she saw an ad in the paper that a positive thinking seminar was being held where she lived. "It was my one and only attempt to better my life," Margot said. And it turned out to be the right one for her.

She bought the seminar books and began to study. A workbook was part of the course, and she did her homework conscientiously. She was rebooting her thinking, slowly realizing that her life was not over. She saw a vision of herself as outgoing, friendly, with lots of friends. "That was too big a vision," she said in a dry tone. So she modified it to being friendly and getting involved in volunteer work. This helped enormously; it took her out of herself.

When she was asked to assist in a fundraiser, she committed herself not only to showing up but also to becoming more outgoing. When she didn't understand something, she asked someone. Yes, she became a little assertive! "I was amazed how friendly people could be," she said, recognizing the importance of a support system.

Over several months she developed the courage to deal with her abusers at work. When a taunt came her way, she would turn around, hold up her pencil and say, "See, I am going to write. Aren't you proud of me?" "That shut them up," she told me in a satisfied tone. Margot realizes that she will never be an extrovert, but she is content with the way she is now and is vigilant not to slip back into her own old way of letting people walk all over her. She has rebooted his life!

Aisha

Aisha's abuse was based on cultural discrimination at the pharmacy where she worked. I met Aisha when I was teaching English as a Second Language at night and was immediately drawn to her. She had a friendly face and expressive eyes, and her interest in learning made her an exceptional student. In her late twenties, Aisha was the only Muslim in my class, dressed in a long-sleeved garment and a scarf, although her face was not covered. We often talked after class when she had to wait for her brother to pick her up.

Aisha told me that she was in the U.S. on a visa and had found work as a clerk in a local pharmacy. She did well in class and wanted to attend college to become a pharmacist. Her present job was a great stepping-stone. She spoke some English but wanted to improve so she could better deal with the public, as well as better communicate with her professors.

One night she confided in me that her work situation was oppressive. Aisha had never told her family about it because they were happy she could bring in some extra money. Her immediate supervisor, Jane, although admitting that Aisha was bright, saw her as someone who would not fit in. Her clothing was different, she adhered to the Muslim religion, and she brought her own lunch!

"Jane's favorite joke is that I might have a bomb under my clothing!" Aisha said. "The other clerks are of course siding with Jane. They all want me to dress like they do, and they pick on me continuously. I like what I am wearing. Why can't they leave me alone?" This, unfortunately, was at a time before I wrote down my five-step strategy to escape abuse.

I asked Aisha if she would like to become "one of the girls," and she responded, "I will never be just like them. Although I would like to have American citizenship, I may want to return to my country later, and I will never abandon my religion."

We didn't have much more time to talk after that. Aisha passed my class with a high grade, and I lost track of her.

Months later I ran into her at an intercultural meeting, and she told me how she had handled her situation. By rebooting her thinking she knew what she had to do. First, she said, she decided to take matters into her own hands. When there was a quiet moment at the pharmacy, she told her fellow employees why she was dressed like she was – that it made her feel safe and secure and that by wearing these clothes she honored her religion. It made the other girls curious, and some of them even wanted to try on her scarf.

"I had this vision," she said, "of us coming together and working together despite our differences." She brought some special foods she had made, favorites in her country, and during lunch she urged the others to taste them. To their surprise most of them liked the food.

She made the commitment to be open to their questions and not to get upset, and she actually began to take pride in her ability to answer them honestly and openly. She stood up for herself and told them, "You dress your way, and I dress my way, but underneath we all are women with the same feelings." And they began to understand that.

"Til, I almost feel like an ambassador. It gives me hope we can work together."

It wasn't long after that that she became even more assertive and asked to be given more responsible work. Jane hesitated at first, but by that time Aisha had won over most of her co-workers and they all supported her. She had changed tormentors into a support system. Aisha had rebooted her life!

She eventually became a U.S. citizen, finished her degree, and became a pharmacist. She had also become a liaison between the community where she lived and her own Muslim community. She decided to be more open than she had been in the past. Today Aisha is a strong, serene Muslim woman with productive ties to both communities. She is married and raises her children in a true international way, believing that we are all one and the same.

Denise

Denise was a young, attractive woman with an engaging smile. She had passed her realtor's exam, and had at one time worked for a large real estate company, hoping to get the training and experience she lacked. However, there was a problem right there in her office. Her broker, Diane, knew that Denise was dreaming of one day owning her own office, but, fearing the competition, gave her no opportunity to learn. Seldom did Diane give her floor duty to pick up any incoming calls, and when Denise did get some, the inquiries were given to more knowledgeable realtors.

She asked for a meeting with her broker and was told that there were plenty of opportunities for her to get experience if she just would apply herself. "Apply myself!" stormed Denise, "All I wanted was to learn and get experience. How can you get it if nobody teaches you how or even lets you work with callers?"

Her boss told her that there were plenty of books lying around in the office. She could take them home and if she had any questions all she had to do was ask the other realtors. However, the others were always busy themselves or joined ranks with the broker, saying she could teach herself. They didn't really care about the newcomer.

Denise got very frustrated and was about to quit when a friend suggested she draw up a five-year plan. How did she see herself at the end of five years? What vision did she have? Could she see herself being a broker? How about the end of the first year? Maybe a smaller vision of selling a few homes? When rebooting her thinking, Denise knew she still wanted to be a realtor. She knew that her warm, outgoing personality attracted people, including possible clients.

She decided to leave that office and spend a few months checking out various other realties. She had joined the large company thinking that it would give her firm footing, but now she knew better. After visiting other real estate companies and checking out the atmosphere at each one, she finally decided on a small office with only a few people. The broker was nice, and he took an interest in her because she was assertive and knew what she wanted. He assigned an experienced realtor to mentor her, which gave her the professional support system she needed.

It was a big surprise when her mentor asked her to sit in on an open house for a couple of hours because he had a prior engagement. She didn't get any prospective clients, but at the end of the month she found an envelope with $200 on her desk as a thank you for covering his open house. "That gave me the necessary push to succeed," Denise said.

She re-committed to her vision. At the end of her first year she had met her goal. She had sold two homes, the second one without any help, and is now well on her way to reaching her five-year goal to get her broker's license. She had rebooted her life.

"You know," she confided, "bigger is not always better. It pays off not to rush into things." She is determined to work hard, hang in there, and make her long-term goal a reality.

Til

The last example of a woman facing abuse in the workplace is my own. I was that woman. My husband and I had arrived in the U.S. during the summer months and had found a small apartment. There wasn't much money. I was alone for much of the day, and when December rolled around I decided to make some extra money so I could buy my husband a couple of shirts as a Christmas present.

I had seen an ad in the local paper that a large department store needed seasonal help so I took the bus downtown and applied for a job. I spoke English reasonably well and was put to work in the accessories department. Little did I know what I was in for!

From the very first moment I met Tara, the head sales lady in the department, she was bound and determined to make trouble for me. When I was busy with a customer, she would rush over, elbow me aside and say to the customer, "She doesn't know anything, she is just temporary, and she can barely speak English!" Sometimes the customer would walk away, but most of them, pressed for time, gladly dealt with her. When I came back from my mid-morning break, she would berate me in front of everybody that I was always late. During the lunch break Tara had her entourage, and I ended up sitting by myself.

Soon I was called on the carpet by the department head and asked why I had not turned in more sales slips. They couldn't keep me on if I didn't sell anything! I now had a choice: take the unwarranted blame or tell on my supervisor. Talk about a dilemma!

But then I had that vision of giving my husband his new shirts on our first Christmas here, and I committed myself to telling the truth in spite of the likely backlash. I told him how I was being discriminated against, how it made me feel, and that

I was constantly being pushed aside and therefore had not been able to write any sales slips. Yes, I had become assertive, not because I wanted to but because I had to. I wanted to buy those shirts! I had to reboot my thinking!

To my great surprise he smiled. He knew all about Tara, he said. She had a reputation, but they kept her on because she was so very good at selling. He wrote something on a slip of paper and told me to report the next morning to a different department. He was my support system. There, at the shoe department, my new supervisor, who was African American, shook my hand and smiled – more support! My spirit was re-energized. Being honest and persevering had paid off. My work life was rebooted.

On Christmas Eve, I was able to give my husband three shirts and a tie bought with my own money!

CONCLUSION

We can draw many lessons from these instances of workplace abuse, but the most important one is to be pro-active, active for yourself.

In their book *The Bully at Work,* Gary and Ruth Namie, each of whom has a Ph.D., chose the following quote to encourage victims of bullies. It's called "Action Is the Antidote" and was written by Ralph Waldo Emerson.

"Whatever you do, you need courage. Whatever course you decide upon, there is always someone to tell you that you are wrong. There are always difficulties arising which tempt you to believe that your critics are right. To map out a course of action and follow it to the end requires some of the same courage which a soldier needs."

Overcoming and escaping the abuse of a bully or bullies in many ways resembles battle. The victim must develop a strategy to overcome the bullying and to maintain the successes permanently. It isn't easy, but it is wonderfully worth the effort.

Chapter Seven

ADULT CHILDREN ABUSING THEIR PARENTS

Parent Abuse is a silent problem, one that exists because people don't often think of abuse as being perpetrated by children against their parents.

Parent Abuse is generally considered to be any act of a child that is intended to cause physical, psychological, or financial damage to gain power and control over a parent. These acts include assault with or without a weapon, emotional manipulation, verbal abuse, and theft.

In this chapter we will discuss the most common type of parental abuse that goes unpunished, yet can be extremely toxic. It is the verbal and emotional abuse perpetrated by adult children against their parents. Words hurt and leave marks. Unfortunately when a mother's child causes emotional damage, the mother often makes no complaint.

Parent abuse can occur in any family regardless of socio-economic class, ethnic background, or sexual orientation. Although fathers are also susceptible, mothers are the most frequent victims of parent abuse. One of the reasons is that women are the primary caregivers. They spend more time with their children than fathers and have closer emotional connections to them. In addition, if only one parent is alive, it is most likely the mother.

Most parents have difficulty accepting the fact that their adult son or daughter is abusive. They often feel depressed, anxious, and ashamed that they "didn't raise the children to behave better." Regaining control begins by acknowledging the problem and then taking the necessary steps, which usually include getting counseling and often distancing oneself from the child. This brings relief, but with it there is also a mixed sense of failure and loss.

The following stories were told to me by parents who have had to deal with the emotional and verbal abuse by their children. With courage and determination they were able to prevail over their younger, but not wiser, kids.

Gerda

Meet Gerda. A widow in her mid-sixties, Gerda had two children, a boy, Anton, and a girl, Stephanie. Both were bright and did well in college. Anton never married and is as close to his mother as ever. Stephanie, however, resented the fact that they were middle-class people and decided to become wealthy – at any cost.

Early in her college years Stephanie saved up for a really gorgeous dress and befriended fellow students who came from well-to-do homes where she would be invited to attend parties. She would show up dressed to kill. People found her witty and charming.

Once inside, Stephanie worked the room. "I am graduating next year with a degree in marketing," she would say. "I would like to intern with your company. Could I have your business card?"

"Stephanie told me she would marry only a doctor, lawyer, or CEO," her mother said wistfully.

Stephanie did well. Her marketing skills were in demand, and within a few years she married a quiet young man who clearly was on an upward path. Today Stephanie has two children, a mansion, and a thriving business of her own.

Gerda and her son Anton are close, but Stephanie visits only sporadically. When she does come, her remarks are derogatory. She criticizes the way Gerda looks after the little house she has, and wants nothing to do with a former childhood friend who lives next door. "I have outgrown her, Mother!" Stephanie snapped.

Gerda was pleased once when she was invited to come and stay for a while. But when she got there, she was nothing more than a cheap babysitter. "Stephanie and her husband were going on a little vacation, which she had neglected to tell me about. Everything nice she did had a string attached."

Eventually the situation became so bad that Gerda had to seek outside help. The minister she turned to for guidance advised her to write a letter to her daughter explaining exactly how she felt. "You have suppressed your feelings all these years," he said, "It is now time to clear the air."

Gerda did just that, but no response ever came. "Never mind," she said, "I feel so much better having done that! I should have done it years ago instead of bottling up all my hurt."

Gerda decided it was time to take her life back and go on living without the constant fear of what her daughter was going to say. She rebooted her thinking and had a vision! She would commit herself to keeping in touch with Stephanie and her family even though they seldom are in touch with her. "I will even send them birthday and Christmas cards. I will stick to the high road," she promised herself. In saying these words and meaning it, she has learned to be assertive and stand up for herself.

The same minister helped her find a group of women in her church who have experienced similar problems, and now Gerda has her own support circle. Today she feels like a new woman because she rebooted her life. She and her newfound friends go out for lunch, meet in each others' homes and support each other when another birthday goes by without a word from their children. She has her own form of vigilance, she says. "I've given it over to God, and I still have Anton."

Judy

Judy was a divorced mother with a son named John, whom she loved dearly. Her dream was that once John was married she would have a wonderful daughter-in-law. She saw herself and the young lady going shopping together, maybe even taking vacations together, and of course she would love the grandchildren.

One day Judy got a phone call from John telling her he had met Maryanne, the girl of his dreams. She was so happy! Maryanne had served four years in the army and sounded wonderful over the phone. Judy was convinced they would hit it off and become close.

When John and Maryanne had their first baby, Judy flew over to see her first granddaughter. She had a hard time remembering how to deal with babies, Judy said, but she figured her daughter-in-law would help her with that. "Imagine my surprise," she said, when after she had been there for just one day, her daughter-in-law inexplicably turned against her, accusing her of being dirty and not paying enough attention to the baby. She even refused to cook for Judy. "I didn't know what to think. I really had no idea what I had done. It was like she was a female Jekyll and Hyde."

Then slowly but surely her own son started withdrawing from her. His wife had effectively drawn a wedge between them and he now openly sided with her whenever his mother was accused of something.

Judy kept on trying, but the abuse kept on coming. On two occasions she stopped to see them on her way to visit another relative. She was hoping things would change, but nothing did. Maryanne barely spoke to her when John was around. But when he left for work and it was just she and her daughter-in-law, the abuse was profound. "I take it you want breakfast before you go. There in the cupboard you can find something." So Judy ate her bowl of cereal in silence and alone, while her granddaughter was still asleep.

"Much as I hated it, all I could do was get out of that house," she said. She decided never to visit them again, hoping to re-connect with her granddaughter later in life.

To this day things are the same. Judy feels she lost not only her dream but her son as well. "I internalized so much of my hurt and sorrow," she said, "that I had to go into therapy. My stomach was in knots, and I couldn't live that way any longer."

After several months of counseling she had a new vision. Like so many mothers in her situation, she had never stood up for herself, always believing in not making a scene.

Now she sees herself as a person in her own right, smart and capable, with lots of friends who have experienced the same thing. She learned that "Children come through you but are not of you," and she is no longer interested in reliving old hurts. Her (now) two granddaughters are in high school and have Facebook pages where Judy writes, committed to establishing relationships with them. "I'm learning the social media," she laughs.

Judy has learned to stand up for herself and be assertive, and is teaching other women to do the same. She does not want to put herself through any more physical and emotional agony. She has rebooted her thinking and thereby rebooted her life. She is content. "Deep down I know I did the right thing," she asserts. "The only time I need to be vigilant is when the holidays roll around and other people are making plans to be with their families. I know I am not alone in this situation by any means, and I am grateful for all the good things I do have."

Estelle

I met Estelle at a party my husband and I attended. There were many guests, but we managed to find a table with a few empty chairs and got into a conversation with a charming woman who was perhaps in her late sixties. She had beautiful gray hair and was impeccably dressed. With her was a good looking man, Joe, younger by at least a decade, and it was obvious that they were very much in love. They were former RVers (that is, they enjoyed traveling in a recreational vehicle), and since my husband and I shared this interest, we clicked and had a pleasant evening.

Sometime during the evening her husband left us to chat with some of his friends. I remarked to Estelle how nice he was, and she was happy to tell us their story.

Estelle's first husband had developed Parkinson's at a relatively young age and she had taken care of him the best she could. However, after many years he succumbed to the disease and Estelle was a widow. Her three children wanted her to come and live with them, but she had lived in her house for so many years and had so many memories that she refused. "I love to play golf," she said. "My friends and I always meet early in the morning for a round. My life is here."

One evening one of her friends invited Estelle to a get-together at her house, and it was there that she met Joe, who would become her second husband. "He was warm, outgoing, and the perfect gentleman," she said. He was a widower himself, childless, and had been alone for several years. "To make a long story short, we hit it off and he proposed to me a year later."

Then the problems began. Estelle's adult children were not at all happy about the fact that their Mom was going to remarry and did their utmost to dissuade her. They accused Joe of being after her money and asked what business their mother had to marry a man who was so much younger. What about the will? Weren't they going to get their promised share? Would Joe get it all?

"They were on my case night and day," Estelle sighed. At first she tried to be patient, understanding it would take time for them to come to grips with the fact that she was going to remarry. "Don't you want me to be happy?" she asked them.

"Yes, of course, Mom, but you can be happy with your memories." Worst of all they would say, "What would Dad say if you married Joe?"

"That did it!" Estelle said forcefully. It was none of their business, and if they didn't stop it, she would disinherit them. She knew that her first husband would so want her to be happy, and Joe was very understanding about the situation. This was the right decision.

The abuse continued, however, and the children began to call Estelle at all hours and make her miserable. She had to make a decision, Joe or her kids. She chose Joe. "I still have a vision that we will once again be a happy family, and I am committed to making it so. But right now, my main goal is to be free from my kids' abuse, and I must be committed to that for the sake of my own health. So Joe, who is rational and is willing to share me with them if they would be willing to share too, comes first. I have made arrangements with my lawyer to change the will."

Estelle was being assertive and standing up for herself. She had rebooted her thinking. "If this abuse doesn't stop, I will leave everything to him. If it does, my kids will have a share of my inheritance."

Estelle had support from her friends. Some of them had remarried, but not everyone had experienced what Estelle had. Some had had some altercations with their children, and some had children who had warmly accepted their new stepparent. Her friends stuck by Estelle and Joe and attended their wedding. Needless to say, none of her children were there.

"I am still willing to keep the lines of communication open," Estelle sighed," but I will not put up with that abuse and Joe won't either. We'll see what happens." Whether friendly relationships are restored or not, Estelle will keep up her vigilance so that she and Joe will never be subject to abuse from the children again. She has rebooted her life.

Mary Lou

Mary Lou and Bill had been married for about twenty years. It had always been an abusive relationship with Bill continually degrading his wife, not only in public but in front of their two children as well.

The older son had been in his teens when the younger son was born. Mary Lou had stayed with Bill, not only because of the children, but because she had been a homemaker for all of their married life. Her self-esteem was already low when they married, and over the years she had come to accept that what she did was always wrong in his eyes. However, she thought she was a good mother given the fact that the older son did well in school and seldom caused a problem.

After twenty-some years of marriage, Bill divorced Mary Lou, and she was on her own for the first time in her life. The older son was in college and she was left with their younger child, now ready for kindergarten. She found a job as a receptionist, used part of the settlement to put a down payment on a small house, and carried on the best she could.

Mary Lou felt bitter about the divorce. Her husband hadn't just left her; he had up and left when she and the children were away visiting relatives, taking many of the household furnishings with him. As the years passed, that wound more or less healed.

What kept upsetting Mary Lou, however, was the fact that Bill took very little notice of their younger son. He had not been very happy when the boy was born and his interest waned more and more as the boy grew older. After an incident when the son had visited his father and had come home deeply unhappy, Mary Lou called Bill and asked him if he would like to come and visit his son in their hometown. They could stay at a hotel and really get to know each other. He refused.

It was beyond Mary Lou's comprehension. How could he be so distant to his own child? It upset her more and more, especially after Bill went to a lawyer and gave up his right to see his son in exchange for being relieved of his child support.

During the next years the relationship between Mary Lou and her older son deteriorated. She kept receiving flaming e-mails from him accusing her of being an uncivilized person and asking why she couldn't she be more polite and friendly to his father. "It just wasn't in me," Mary Lou said.

She told me about the time she invited her son for Sunday dinner. The answer was "I won't spoil my Sunday." When Mary Lou had her 60th birthday, she invited her son as well as her many friends. The next day she got a phone call from him. "You know, Mother," he said, "I noticed that you looked a little older since I saw you last. I think it is time you get your papers in order, but I want to tell you not to count on me to take care of you. You're on your own." She felt so alone and abandoned, she sobbed.

A light bulb came on when she talked about her problems with a good friend who had had similar experiences with her children. "You know, Til, it suddenly became clear to me," she said. "Both of my two eldest children had grown up with their father abusing me. That's all they ever saw – and me *taking it!* Their father had accused her of being uncivilized and unmannered. No wonder they perpetuated the abuse and, of course sided with the strong one, the one they saw as being right, their dad."

That was the moment Mary Lou knew she had to take action! She rebooted her thinking and suddenly had a vision of herself as a woman who had gone through hell but had come out if it stronger than ever.

It's never too late to change! Mary Lou put a picture of a person she admired on her refrigerator and committed herself to never allowing her older son and her ex-husband to have any influence on her.

She further committed to this vision by taking classes in raising one's self-esteem and voraciously reading books on self-improvement. She changed her image and told her beautician exactly how she wanted her hair done instead of letting the beautician decide. She even had her eyelids lifted!

She became assertive all right. Hurray, she had rebooted her life! She also had the courage to tell her older son she was stepping out of his life.

"I just couldn't take his abuse anymore," she said.

Mary Lou now volunteers her time as a tutor in the local schools and is gratified when she sees how much progress her students make.

She feels supported not only by friends with similar experiences, but also by her younger son with whom she has a close relationship. She believes that because he was so young when she was still married to his father, he never absorbed the abuse that was going on and therefore sees her as she truly is – a warm and caring person and a great mother!

Mary Lou is still vigilant. She says, "It is so easy to slip back into the old behavior patterns. I still tend to think of myself now and then as an unworthy person, but that quickly dissipates when I look at myself, attractive, outgoing, and doing something I always wanted to do – helping others!"

Margaret

When I met Margaret and Mark, they had been married for many years and were both in their late eighties. They had one daughter, Mary, who had moved in with them when she lost her job and her condo. It was a big adjustment on their part but, Margaret sighed, "What are you going to do when your daughter is homeless?"

Mary had never married and was a surly woman who chain-smoked. Boundaries were set, however, amid much shouting, and Mary was allowed to smoke only outside the house. She kept to herself and finally found a job as a waitress at a local restaurant.

Mark's health deteriorated and he was diagnosed with Alzheimer's disease. Margaret tried to keep an eye on him when he started to wander off, but she had difficulty walking herself and enlisted her neighbors to watch out for him as well. "I had so hoped that Mary would be able to help me, but all she did was sit and watch TV when she came home from her part-time job. I tried to tell her I could use some help around the house, but she said she was working and I wasn't so why should she bother! I thought that she should be grateful she could stay in our home and not have to pay a dime."

Things got worse over time. One evening Mark got upset with all the bickering and shouting. He didn't know where he was anymore. Margaret tried to calm him down but ended up crying, and so he got upset again.

Meanwhile Mary was shouting at them both. Finally she told them what a horrible parents they both were and threatened to "tell everything to the neighbors." During her shouting spree she managed to break some china and struck Margaret in the face. Then she went to her room, slamming the door.

Margaret didn't know what to do anymore, but she did know that her first responsibility was to Mark. She tried to ignore her daughter and carried on the best she could.

A few months later Mark died in his sleep. Many people came to the funeral, but Mary was not among them. "Actually," Margaret said, "I was relieved. It would only have upset me more to see her sitting there." Margaret took comfort from the fact that so many of her friends were in attendance.

Finally things began to change. For the first time in her life Margaret took a long, hard look at her daughter; she rebooted her thinking, and saw her for the rude, self-centered woman she really was. It shocked her, she said, because as a parent one tends to turn a blind eye.

She envisioned having her life back and regaining a certain measure of freedom now that Mark was gone. She was not about to let her remaining years be ruined by her daughter.

She committed herself to restore peace and quiet to the house, being able to watch her favorite TV shows, and doing some things with her friends.

"It took me a while," Margaret smiled, "but I managed to rustle up enough courage to face Mary. I told her bluntly that it was either shape up or ship out. And since she had little money of her own, I knew she would prefer to stay here. I laid down rules about helping around the house and respecting me." Margaret was being assertive and standing up for herself!

"I am committed to sticking to my decisions and feel so much better about having made them. I have friends galore who know what kind of person Mary is, and who Support me completely. I do have to watch myself though. Mary can be terribly overbearing, and I am old. It wouldn't take much to have the situation reversed again, but I am determined to stick to my guns and remain vigilant against backsliding."

I saw Margaret again several months later and asked how things were going. "I'm hanging in there," she said. "Mary's behavior has improved and best of all she has found an extra job. I'm now going to ask her to contribute to the household!" Hurray for Margaret! She has rebooted her life.

CONCLUSION:

Parents who are abused by adult children must realize they have the choice to not tolerate deplorable treatment. They do not have to submit to their children's abuses, just because they think they may not have raised them the right way. I used to believe that, but, now I believe that there are two ways to view this type of abuse. One is that children can learn hurtful, abusive behaviors from other people, e.g., another parent, a sibling, kids at school, teachers, or others who are in a leadership or control role. Children are impressionable, and may adopt inappropriate behaviors for any number of reasons. But you don't have to tolerate them, whatever the source.

Second, some children are simply born with an abusive temperament that may increase as they grow and mature. They came into the world that way, and might remain that way without intervention and treatment. Like Judy, you may choose to believe that "children come through you, but are not of you." They have simply developed their own way of thinking.

Parents can develop their strength by re-building their sense of self-worth. This often begins with a vision. How would I like my life to be? Will I commit to this vision? Will I become assertive enough to stand up for myself? This might mean distancing myself from my child. Who can I count on to support my choices?

Realize that you will have to be vigilant. It is so easy to pick up the phone and say, "I'm sorry, this is all my fault." But you must not give in. Will you be able to do that? I believe you can.

Keep this in mind. Adult children need to realize that they still have parents who are entitled to be treated with courtesy if not respect. Yelling seems a normal recourse in arguing, but yelling can turn into abuse, and you do *not* have to put up with that!

Muster your strength. Reread the above stories of abused parents. You know in your head that you, like every human being, are worthy of being treated well. Say it out loud and repeat it often. Make it become a part of your soul, too.

Chapter Eight

SEXUAL ABUSE

I have long hesitated to write a chapter on sexual abuse since the preceding chapters deal exclusively with emotional and verbal abuse. However, since so many women have shared with me their experiences of being sexually assaulted, and it is part of my life as well, I decided to address this elephant in the room.

Ellen Bass and Laura Davis have written a book on abuse called *The Courage to Heal*. In it they write:

If you have been sexually abused, you are not alone. One out of three girls and one out of seven boys are sexually abused by the time they reach the age of eighteen. Sexual abuse happens to children of every class, culture, race, religion, and gender. Children are abused by fathers, stepfathers, uncles, brothers, grandparents, neighbors, family friends, babysitters, teachers, strangers, and sometimes by aunts and mothers (and others).

Although women do abuse, the vast majority of abusers are heterosexual men.

All sexual abuse is damaging, and the trauma does not end when the abuse stops. If you were abused as a child, you are probably experiencing long-term effects that interfere with your day-to-day functioning.

How can I know if I was sexually abused as a child? Were you:

- Touched in sexual areas?

- Shown sexual movies or forced to listen to sexual talk?

- Made to pose for seductive or sexual pictures?

- Forced to perform oral sex on an adult or sibling?

- Raped or otherwise penetrated?

- Fondled, kissed, or held in a way that made you uncomfortable?

- Forced to take part in ritualized abuse in which you were physically or sexually tortured?

- Made to watch sexual acts or look at sexual parts?

- Bathed in a way that felt intrusive to you?

- Objectified and ridiculed about your body?

- Encouraged or goaded into sex you didn't really want?

- Told all you were good for was sex?

- Involved in child prostitution or pornography?

If you can say "yes" to any of the above, you were sexually abused.

The following stories reveal how women who were sexually abused were able to pick up the pieces and move on.

Terry

Terry's parents married when her mother was 18 years old and her father 31. Her mother was attractive in a boyish sort or way, and did not have what we would call a feminine figure. They had two daughters, Margie and, four years later, Terry. The parents often argued with each other, and the age difference didn't help. Terry said, "They were two angry people."

When she was very young, Terry was molested, not only by her father and grandfather, but also by a friend who babysat the girls. Terry never confided in her sister or her mother, though she knew her sister had been molested as well. She was so mixed up. She loved her grandfather and her father, and had been told by the friend that her father said it was okay. After all, he was practically a member of the family. "They said they did it because they loved me so much," Terry continued bitterly.

This situation continued for many years, and Terry and her sister developed into beautiful girls. "My father's preference was for girls who had a feminine figure," she said in a dry tone. Still more damaging was the fact that their mother knew about the abuse. She was just glad her husband preferred Terry and her sister, so that she wouldn't be bothered. Margie moved out of the house when she turned sixteen, leaving Terry to deal with her problems alone. She remembers not being allowed to join any clubs or go to sleepovers, and she became an introverted, lonely young girl.

Terry chose to escape, however, by going to college, about six hours away from home, but quit, too depressed to succeed. Because moving back home was not an option, she had to support herself. Fortunately the college offered her a secretarial position.

"I didn't think about my childhood," she said. "I had absolutely no memories of the abuse, they were so deeply buried." She never called her parents, preferring to live her own life.

After six years Terry met her first husband. Things would be better, she thought, and she had a vision of going back to school and finishing her teaching degree. She discovered, however, that her husband was abusive, and the marriage ended in divorce.

Then Terry developed a new vision. After hitting rock bottom when her husband left, she wanted to become whole. She went for counseling, and all her suppressed memories slowly started to come back.

"It was very difficult," she said, "I sobbed, screamed, and hit out at whatever was handy, I felt I was drowning in pain but it had to come out!"

Terry rebooted her thinking and made the commitment to stick with the therapy, but it took months to come to grips with the early years of her life. Finally she became assertive enough to stand up for herself, and called her mother. She learned that her mother had died of cancer a few years earlier and that her father had developed Alzheimer's disease. Then Terry called her sister. Margie was surprised to hear from her and, when questioned about their early years, vehemently denied she was ever raped. "But I knew better. She was still in denial after all these years!"

In her late 40s Terry hooked up with a man through a dating service. Again, she lived with an abuser, but this time she knew how to stand up for herself. She walked out on him, taught for a few more years, and then started her own business through sheer determination. She was able to reboot her life!

Today she is content to be alone but is not lonely because she has joined some rewarding organizations and has made supportive friends. She remains vigilant, however, because "Once you have been molested like I was, even though you can rise above it, it still stays with you."

Fran

Fran was a naïve young girl, 13 years old. She was the only child of parents who strictly adhered to the old-fashioned way of marriage. Her father was an autocratic man who laid down the law in his house, and her mother was subservient to all his demands. She dreaded her husband's violent outbursts but wrote it all off to his business concerns.

Once a week Fran visited her Aunt Beth who lived about a half-hour walk away. She enjoyed the little journey and looking at the various shops as she was walked along to her aunt's assisted living building.

Fran loved being with Aunt Beth. She always had cookies and hot chocolate, and Fran would tell her all she had done each week. It made her feel special that someone paid so much attention to her.

One week, the weather was nasty and cold as Fran returned from her visit. All bundled up and warmed inside by hot chocolate and with some cookies in her pocket, she pushed toward home. Then it started to rain.

There were apartment buildings she had to pass that were entered by going up a short flight of stairs. When she got near the first building, she heard a noise. Looking up she saw a man standing at the bottom of the entry steps. He was beckoning to her and, naïve as Fran was, she went over to him. He explained he needed some help and, as Fran was a kind girl, she immediately asked what she could do.

They went up the entry steps together, and before she knew what was going on, he had exposed himself and ordered her to hold his penis in her hand while he ejaculated. Scared, Fran did as she was told and then ran out as fast as she could.

When she got home, she told her mother about it. Instead of immediately calling the police, her mother told her not to say a word to anyone about it – "People wouldn't believe you anyway" – and certainly not to her father because "he would be so angry."

Fran mentioned it once to a girlfriend who didn't believe her, and so Fran thought that her mother was right and never brought it up again.

Then when she was older, her uncle fondled and kissed her. This time, when she told her mother, the answer was, "Not again, surely?" and she glossed over it.

Fran learned to bury her feelings of outrage, and over the years began to see sex as something dirty and shameful. She said that it has always hindered her in her relationships. She found herself being "happiest" when she was left alone, and she started drinking, in time becoming an alcoholic. Fran wanted to escape from the life she had created and finally had the courage to join AA. She has been sober for several years.

Marriage didn't appeal to Fran until later in life when she finally found a man she liked; however, sex was still a problem for her. In the beginning her husband accused her of being an "ice queen" until she trusted him enough to tell him what had happened. He recommended that she talk things over with a counselor. Fran took his advice and began to see herself in a new light. The realization finally hit her that nothing that had happened had been her fault. That's when she rebooted her thinking!

She formed a vision of herself as a complete, healthy woman. She committed herself to being open to her husband, and he encouraged her to talk about her feelings when they were intimate. He supported her in ways that on one ever had.

Today Fran values herself as the woman she is, capable of receiving and giving, and asserting herself. She told me that, because she was afraid to lose a husband she knew was wonderful, she was willing to do whatever it took to overcome her past, and to remain vigilant so that thoughts of her past can't bring down what she worked hard to build.

"It was difficult for me to open up to my husband and to a therapist," she said. "I was so used allowing the anger and shame to shut me down and just let things happen. But now I'm glad I did it. We have a great marriage and great sex. I couldn't have married a better or more understanding guy." She has successfully rebooted her life.

Kathy

Kathy came from a poor family and was one of six siblings. The village she grew up in consisted of some 80-plus homes, mostly farms, and there was just a one-room schoolhouse for kindergarten through eighth grade. The schoolhouse had a spacious apartment attached to it and a large vegetable garden. Kathy's home was close to the school, separated from it by a dirt path surrounded by bushes which then opened up into pasture. Kathy liked the teacher she had for the first three years, but then unfortunately he moved away.

Finally a new teacher arrived. He had a wife and two babies and was well liked by everyone. He could whittle little animals from wood and taught the children music. Kathy said she saw him as the most accomplished man she had ever met!

Home life was not the best for Kathy. Her mother could not always handle all her children and handed discipline out fast and furious. Her father was a traveling salesman and was mostly absent.

Kathy gloried in the fact that her new teacher thought she was cute, and she did well in school. He always praised her for her efforts, which was great, she said, because her mother paid very little attention to them.

It wasn't long before he asked her if she would babysit for his two children after school while he wrote lesson plans. Their mother had a job as well and would often not be home before six in the evening. Kathy's mother immediately agreed. It would bring in more money, and Kathy was beside herself with joy! Now she would be in the same house with her beloved teacher! She was eight years old when she started to babysit. It was an easy job. After all she was one of six and she knew how to change diapers and feed babies.

Then it started. When the babies slept, he came out of his office and raped her brutally, telling her it was a game just for the two of them. "You know you're my favorite student, don't you?" he asked. She adored him so much that she let him, even though she hurt badly in the beginning. Sometimes he brought her home when it was dark in the winter and raped her in the bushes not far from her house. She never told her parents, afraid they wouldn't believe her. He was the teacher, after all!

The abuse continued for six years. "You know what was the worst, Til?" she asked. "After I was a little older, my body started to mature, and started to respond to his raping me!" It didn't hurt anymore, and my body simply responded to the stimuli."

After eighth grade Kathy left her village and finished her education in a convent school.

She eventually married and ended up in an abusive relationship in which her husband threatened to take the children away from her if she didn't do as she was told. Oh, she longed to escape, but at the time she didn't have the courage.

Life was so difficult that at one point she decided to kill herself. She closed the bathroom door and was ready to slit her wrists when an enormous anger came over her. She cried out against the rapes, the abuse, all the hurt she had ever felt. She had a vision of a better life away from her husband and made the decision to reboot her thinking. She suddenly felt empowered by assertiveness and the drive to stand up for herself. She went to her husband and told him point-blank she was leaving.

He just stared at her, open-mouthed. This was not a Kathy he knew.

She packed her belongings, took her two small children, found an apartment, and started divorce proceedings. She was committed to a new and positive future for herself and her children. Of course she was granted custody of the children.

"My life has not been easy since the divorce," she said, "but the vision in that bathroom showed me that that was not how life should be lived. Now I have two good friends who support me and I am grateful for every new day. I have learned to forgive my body. Its reactions to the rape were not its fault.

I get counseling when I can afford it, but I know that if I'm vigilant, the past will remain just that, the past. I am a strong woman who will find her way. Divorcing my husband was the best thing I ever did." Yes, she has rebooted her life!

Thinking back, she tells me, "You know, my teacher's wife knew her husband was a pedophile. Why else would such an accomplished man, an artist, take a teaching job in such a backwater village? He could have had any position he wanted. I believe he was kicked out of several jobs and ended up there where no one would know him. How could she let that go on!"

There are many ways to be violated. As you will see from the following stories, it doesn't have to be rape or incest.

Sandra

Sandra grew up in the suburbs of New York. Her mother was an administrative assistant and her father had his own business. And she had a brother named Keith. Both parents valued education and had their children tested at an early age.

Sandra was found to be extremely bright and Keith of average intelligence. He was never a problem and he became a happy-go-lucky guy. He liked sports, did his homework, often in a slapdash way, went to school regularly, and had many friends. Sandra, on the other hand, was rather quiet and sensitive, and read a lot after she finished her homework. The siblings got along but went their separate ways.

Sandra's parents were advised to put her in a special high school where she could progress at her own pace and graduate one or two years earlier than the average child. Of course her parents were delighted and scraped the money together for Sandra to go to that high school. The best colleges would then be open to her. The trouble was that the school was quite a distance from her home and she had to take the subway each day to get to class.

Sandra was tall for her age and with her long blond hair and in her new school uniform she made a striking picture.

One morning as she was on her way to school, a man sitting across from her, lifted his newspaper a few inches. To her horror she saw that his zipper was open and his penis was clearly visible. He smiled at her, lowered his paper again and said nothing.

When the train stopped at her station, she was ready to get out as fast as possible, but there were too many passengers and she had to wait. The man managed to stand right behind her, and all of a sudden Sandra felt something rammed hard between her buttocks. She was afraid to cry out, and she was hemmed in by people and couldn't move.

Finally she stepped outside onto the platform, but her assailant was right behind her and grabbed her arm, linking it into his own. Together they walked out towards the elevator which would bring them to street level – the man with a briefcase and overcoat looking as if he were escorting his daughter. There were masses of people everywhere and, of course, no police in sight. On the elevator up he was right behind her and again he pushed his penis between her buttocks. Once on the street, she ran over to a policeman and described the incident. Looking around, she realized she was alone; the man had vanished into the crowd.

Of course there was nothing to be done. When she described the incident to her friends at school, they looked at her as if that was nothing out of the ordinary. "You're on a subway," they told her, "What can you expect? It happens to us all sometimes." She told her parents about the incident, but they insisted she stay in that school. It was her future at stake and no harm had been done. "In short, they wanted me to just get over it," Sandra said bitterly.

However, Sandra couldn't let it go. She became afraid to take the subway. When a man sat across from her, she moved away to a seat where she felt safe. Later it became a phobia that forced her to take taxis wherever she went. She knew she needed to escape from this obsession, but it took years to resolve.

Slowly, as the time passed, she rebooted her thinking and developed a vision of herself being able to function in a big city, including taking the subway. She committed herself to counseling, which helped her overcome her phobia. She developed her assertiveness and took her first ride in a subway in a long time, accompanied by her counselor.

Today Sandra is a respected psychologist with a specialty in women's abuse. She also belongs to several counseling organizations. They form her support group. However, even after all these years, the incident stays with her. "He made me feel so helpless," she said.

She uses that feeling to fuel her vigilance. It shows itself through the care she lavishes on her clients. "It gives me such empathy for them," she says. She, too, was successful in rebooting her life.

Til

The last story is about me. Again I stress that you don't have to be raped or sexually assaulted to be sexually abused.

When I was about 12 years old, I was walking our dog near a brook, not far from my home, when I spotted one of the older boys from my school sitting at the edge of the water and fishing. He was a mean kid who made fun of me, and of many others. I couldn't very well avoid him by turning around, because that would really give him some ammunition to talk about in school! So I stuck it out.

I didn't say hello when I got close to him, hoping that if I ignored him he would keep his mouth shut. I had just drawn abreast of him, pulling on the leash to hurry my dog along, when all of a sudden he raised his fishing pole and poked it repeatedly in my genital area, laughing out loud. I swept the pole out of the way, scared and angry, and continued on my way home without saying a word.

It burned where he had poked me and when I looked at my panties when I got home, there was a little blood. I felt demeaned and scared and my already low self-esteem took a nosedive. I never told my parents, but my fear intensified every time I saw him. Because he went to the same school I did, all I could think about was how he must have bragged to his friends and that everyone now knew what had happened!

Another sexually related incident happened later, when I was in high school. Two popular girls invited me to go by train to another city to attend a swim meet. They were groupies of a Yugoslavian swim team and, unknown to me, fully intended to sleep with a couple of the members after the meet. I was very pleased to have been invited and of course went with them. They told me what I should say and do. This was to be my initiation! I was very uneasy but wanted to be "just like them," so I agreed.

We sat together and rooted for the foreign team, and they won. Afterward three guys came up to us, in very brief swimming trunks that left nothing to the imagination, and we split up. The other two girls disappeared with their two guys, and I was left with a young man with friendly eyes. He must have seen how scared I was because he suggested we go to the zoo, bless him.

On the way home the girls asked me if I had "made out." When I told them we had gone to the zoo, they burst out laughing. They continued to whisper to each other and look at me, the innocent. Needless to say I was the butt of jokes later in class.

"Did you enjoy the zoo, Til?" they taunted. "Did you see the monkeys?"

Fast forward to my late teens. I was a tour guide showing American children around in my country. They came by bus from Germany accompanied by chaperones and a photographer. Often there was a certain Hungarian photographer on board, a very good-looking man. He took pictures not only of the children but also of me.

One day I was invited for the weekend to stay with one of the American families in Germany. While I was there, the photographer showed me around and, innocent as I was, I promptly fell in love with him. That night, while my hosts were away, he brought me home and promptly tried to make love to me. I refused to take my clothes off so he just lay on top of me, thrusting his penis against me again and again. Of course, just at that time, my hosts came home!

The wife let out a scream and told him to get out. The next morning I found that a note had been slipped under my bedroom door. I was told that I was no longer welcome and that a friend of theirs had agreed to let me stay with her for the rest of the weekend.

Breakfast was laid out for me. I ate in silence, packed, and was picked up by their friend. The fact that my first hostess had automatically blamed me for the whole thing made me feel small and shameful. Fortunately her friend was more understanding and took me shopping. The next day I rode the bus back to the Netherlands and never told my parents.

Fast forward again to my adult years. One day when I was married to my second husband, we had company over. While I was serving them coffee, I turned around to get some things from the kitchen, and my husband stuck his well-polished shoe between my thighs. I was mortified but he just laughed. Our guests pretended not to notice.

So you see, rape and incest are not required to make a woman feel small and demeaned in a sexual way. An accumulation of sexual abuse can have the same effect. It made me feel like someone who could be taken advantage of at any time and any place. I came to see sex as something shameful, something people did on the sly. It took a good while in therapy in later years to make me into a whole person. I rebooted my thinking, but the scars will never go away.

My vision today is to speak out against abuse, anywhere and anytime, and I have committed myself to doing just that. I learned to be assertive and to stand up for myself by telling my story and having a circle of friends, my support system, who have been sexually abused as well. We support one another.

I have rebooted my life, but I have to be vigilant at all times, and I work at remaining positive. It is very easy to slip back into the old ways of thinking, of seeing oneself as dirty, unworthy, full of shame. All due to someone else's actions.

CONCLUSION

In closing this chapter I would like to tell you that it wasn't easy for me to write it or for the lovely women who shared with me what happened to them to tell it. Sexual abuse is a very private thing, and I want to thank them for the courage they had to come forward so that you could benefit from their experiences.

Look again at the following points. If you were:

- Touched in sexual areas
- Shown sexual movies or forced to listen to sexual talk
- Made to pose for seductive or sexual pictures
- Subjected to unnecessary medical treatment

- Forced to perform oral sex on an adult or another child
- Raped or otherwise penetrated
- Fondled, kissed, or held in a way that made you uncomfortable
- Forced to take part in ritualized abuse in which you were physically or sexually tortured
- Made to watch sexual acts or look at sexual parts
- Bathed in a way that felt intrusive to you
- Objectified and ridiculed about your body
- Encouraged or goaded into sex you didn't really want
- Told all you were good for was sex
- Involved in child prostitution or pornography

then you were sexually abused.

Reboot your thinking. If you follow the 5 steps, you *can* reboot your life.

In Closing

As Ellen Bass and Laura Davis wrote in *The Courage to Heal,* escaping the grip of abuse is not a simple task.

> "Moving on is a tricky business for survivors. It cannot be rushed or pressured. People will tell you to forget it, to 'let the past be the past.' But moving on to please someone else will not help you. Authentic moving on is a natural result of going through each step of the healing process. It comes slowly for some or it catches you by surprise for others."

Moving on means saying, "Yes, I can!" You recognize your own vision and you commit yourself to making it a reality. You stand up for yourself, for what you know to be true. You find someone supportive who will sustain you on this path. Lastly, you are willing to do whatever it takes to be vigilant against the return of people and feelings that destroy what you have worked so hard to build up.

If you follow this 5-step process, you will be able to join the people in this book who didn't like how their life experiences had messed up their thinking and decided to escape.

These abused people started out like you, having no idea that they could escape to a better life. But they thought about it, and they finally accepted the fact that they, like everyone else, deserved to be treated with dignity. Starting from that position, they rebooted their thinking about what their lives had the right to be. Today they value how far they've come and are diligent about their vigilance because going back is not an option. They rebooted their lives.

It worked for them, and it can work for you. Form your vision. Commit to it. Become assertive. Find your support system. Once you have escaped from the negative thinking and negative place your mind knew before, be vigilant against backsliding. You must remember that you are not alone. There are millions of other women who suffer from memories, shame, and anger very much like yours. Why? Because abusers make their victims feel like everything is their fault. *It isn't.*

Know that you have the right to be your own person, with your own opinions and the right to go where and with whom you wish. You have the right to be your Self.

There is a way out of the turmoil you are experiencing. Read and re-read the steps so that they can help you believe in the power of your new knowledge.

Reboot your thinking, and reboot your life.

*You **can** do it. **So do** it.*

BIBLIOGRAPHY

American Justice Department. Child and School
    Bullying Statistics, "School Crime and Safety," 2001.

Bass, Ellen and Laura Davis. *The Courage to Heal.*
    New York: HarperCollins, 2008.

Bully OnLine. http://www.Bullyonline.org. "Child
    Bullying and School Bullying."

CASA (Community Action Stops Abuse).
    St. Petersburg, Florida. www.casa-stpete.org

CASA (Court Appointed Special Advocate).
    www.casaforchildren.org

EWA (Education Wife Assault). North York,
    Ontario, Canada.

Mental Health Matters.
    http://www.Mental-Health-Matters.com. "Myths
    About Emotional and Verbal Abuse." 1998-2010.

King, Jeanne, Ph.D. "Learn the Truth About Spousal
    Abuse and Domestic Violence."
    http://www.preventabusiverelationships.com

Lutgen-Sandvik, Pamela, Ph.D., Tracy, S. J., and Alberts, J. K. "Burned by Bullying in the American workplace: Prevalence, Perception, Degree, and Impact." *Journal of Management Studies, 44*(6), 2007.

Marsh, Jaimee, et al. "Prevalence of Workplace Abuse and Sexual Harassment Among Female Faculty and Staff." *Journal of Occupational Health,* 2009.

Namie, Gary, Ph.D. and Ruth Namie, Ph.D. *The Bully at Work: What You Can Do To Stop the Hurt and Reclaim Your Dignity on the Job.* Naperville: Sourcebooks, Inc., 2009.

National Institute of Justice. "Extent, Nature and Consequences of Intimate Partner Violence." July 2001.

Pitner, C. Ronald, Ph.D. "Anti Bullying and School Safety." July 8, 2009.

Wendland, Gary. "Parent Abuse, The Silent Crime." Nov. 21, 2006.

Wetherington, Crista E., Ph.D. Children's Medical Center, Dallas Texas.

RESOURCES

CASA (Community Action Stops Abuse)
St. Petersburg, Florida (727-828-1269)
Web: www.casa-st.pete.org

The Haven of RCS
Clearwater, Florida (727-442-4128)
Web: www.rcspinellas.org

Mary and Martha House, Inc.
Ruskin, Florida (813-641-7027)

National Childrens' Abuse hotline
1-800-4-A-Child (1-800-422-4453)
Web: www.childhelp.org

National Domestic Violence hotline
(1-800-799-7233) (TTY: 1-800-787-3224)
Web: www.thehotline.org

The Spring of Tampa Bay, Inc.
Tampa, Florida (813-247-5433)
Web: www.thespring.org